Complete Guide To

KODACHROME II

by Patricia Caulfield

Universal Photo Books
New York, N. Y.

Contents

ACKNOWLEDGMENTS

Many, many thanks to Herbert Keppler, Edward Meyers, Myron A. Matzkin, Norman Rothschild and Bennett Sherman for sharing with me their extensive knowledge of photographic practice and technique in general as well as the specific results of their own exhaustive tests of Kodachrome II film; to *Modern Photography* magazine, for whom my initial tests of Kodachrome II were undertaken, and for the permission to use the photographs in the color section; to *Photo Methods for Industry* magazine for the permission to run their technical analysis of Kodachrome II in Chapter 10; to Eastman Kodak Company for two photographs on the first page of the color section, for supplying technical data and charts, and for their help in checking the manuscript for technical accuracy.

CHAPTER ONE

Why Kodachrome II

It wasn't until 1936, almost one hundred years after the invention of photography, that a simple system for producing color photographs, in one shot on a single piece of film, became widely available. In that year Kodachrome film, invented by Leopold Mannes and Leopold Godowsky, was marketed by the Eastman Kodak Co. The color barrier was broken, and the photographer, professional or amateur, could make color transparencies just as easily as was indicated by the original Eastman slogan, "You push the button, we do the rest."

Kodachrome film was first marketed in a variety of film sizes: 8 x 10, 4 x 5, 120, 35mm, 16mm and 8mm. I had the opportunity just a few weeks ago of examining some of the early 8 x 10 transparencies shot by one of America's leading commercial photographers. I was astonished by their sharpness, the clarity and seemingly undiminished brilliance of their colors, the delicacy of the detail they recorded, and the full range of tones and hues represented.

The characteristics and quality of the film as originally produced hold true for the Kodachrome manufactured today: it is superior to all subsequent films in sharpness, in lack of grain, in brilliance of color.

The original Kodachrome was of course followed by other color films for the general public. Ansco put out Ansco Color film in 1942, which was soon followed by Eastman Kodak's Ektachrome. Today, in transparency films, we have Anscochrome and Super Anscochrome, in both daylight and tungsten types, and Ektachrome and High Speed Ektachrome, color balanced for shooting by daylight or by artificial light as well as other films made in the U.S.: Dynacolor, DuPont, and films from Europe and Japan. These films are all excellent for various purposes. Most are of a higher speed than Kodachrome, and therefore prove particularly valuable for photographers whose primary purpose is capturing fast action. Because of the construction of many of them, the development procedure is much less complex than that required for Kodachrome and such factors as time and temperature do not require nearly such stringent control.

The amateur can, if he chooses, develop either Anscochrome or Ektachrome and their faster brothers himself; he can try altering development for experimental color effects. Both Anscochrome and Ektachrome can be exposed at higher-than-normal or lower-than-normal indexes, and with altered development can have the characteristic color balance relatively changed. The practice of underexposing and changing development times is widespread among fashion and commercial photographers, since it gives some of the special effects they seek. Extreme pushing of films, while not common, can be done to produce extreme grain, creating an experimental effect similar to the pointillism of some modern painters.

Despite their advantages for a number of purposes, none of these color films measures up to Kodachrome in quality. And now we have a new film, Kodachrome II in 35mm, 828, 16mm and 8mm sizes, which is even sharper and less grainy than the original material (incidentally, Kodachrome is still available and will be in the forseeable future), is 1½ to 2 stops faster, and has even more natural color! Let's look briefly at the construction of a Kodachrome slide for the explanation of its superior quality.

All modern color films are composed of separate emulsion layers, each of which records light of one color only. The original Kodachrome film consisted of three emulsion layers: the uppermost, blue-sensitive layer followed by a yellow dye filter layer which filtered out blue; and two other emulsion layers, recording green and red respectively. When the film is exposed in a camera, light-sensitive silver halides in each layer record that portion of the original scene which is in the color corresponding to its sensitivity. The film is

6

developed to a negative. On the subsequent steps it is reversed into a positive by re-exposure to light. The dyes which produce the colored image you see in your transparency are included in the processing solutions, not "locked" in the separate emulsion layers during film manufacture, as is the case with other color processes. For this reason, there is less "clumping" which produces the apparent grain that can sometimes be perceived in other color films. The Kodachrome image is always smooth and continuous, and will take gigantic blowups without any apparent loss in sharpness or quality.

Kodachrome II is similar to Kodachrome in construction, but is more complex, having several additional layers. But since each emulsion layer is thinner, Kodachrome II is sharper (see chapter 10).

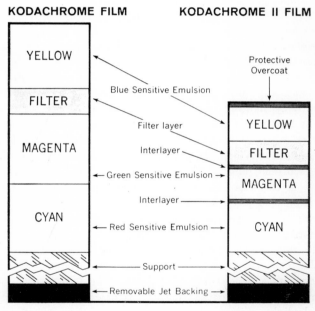

CROSS-SECTIONS of regular and new film show comparative thinness of Kodachrome II. In current production, average thickness of new film is 5.75 mils compared to 6 mils for regular Kodachrome. The support is thicker in relation to the emulsion than shown on the drawing, but emulsion layers are in scale.

In addition, all three dyes have been improved, which in turn means improved color rendition. Now, greens are greener, yellows are yellower, and skies, instead of the intense, almost cyan-blue which we have come to anticipate, are much nearer to the clear, paler color of nature. I was amazed when running color tests, simultaneously shooting Kodachrome and Kodachrome II frame for frame in half stops with a pair of matched Leica M3s, at the difference in color rendition between the two films. After working with Kodachrome for a period of years, I had come to expect, say, a yellow lemon to have a touch of orange. Without a frame of reference, orange yellows had come to appear normal. When projecting equivalently exposed Kodachrome side by side with Kodachrome II, the slightly inaccurate color cast of the former became obvious.

More important, actually than the difference in color between the films is the difference in speed. According to Eastman Kodak Co., the exposure index for Kodachrome II Daylight Type is 25; for Kodachrome II Type A the exposure index recommended is 40. My tests, and those of other photographers as well as all of the photographic magazines, indicated that the film was actually underrated. The recommended exposure index is correct only when shooting in the most contrasty lighting conditions, such as, say, when making a portrait by the light of a single direct flood, or when shooting against the light on a brilliantly sunny day. Ordinarily Kodachrome II Daylight Type can safely be rated at E.I. 32, one and one half stops faster than Kodachrome; and in flat light, it can be rated at E.I. 40, two stops or four times as fast as Kodachrome. Kodachrome II Type A can be rated at E.I. 60 in any but the most contrasty light. This added film speed makes a big difference if, for example, you are photographing a fast-moving ball game, and can shoot at 1/250 second to stop action instead of at 1/60; or if you are trying to render sharp two objects which are on different distance planes from the camera and you need increased depth of field. If you are working by available light, the added speed is of even more importance than in daylight. With Kodachrome II you can shoot well lighted indoor sports events without flash, or you can make candid portraits in your own living room without even boosting the existing illumination.

There is another important characteristic of this film which is connected with its differing speeds in the different types of illumination just mentioned. The original Kodachrome film was of high contrast. Shadows, if the lighting was contrasty, often went completely black if the highlights and middle tones were correctly exposed. If, on the other hand, you chose to expose for the shadows, middle tones would seem too light, and highlights would be completely burned out. This is not quite the case with Kodachrome II. Kodachrome II is less contrasty, and will help to record detail in both highlights and shadows.

Kodachrome II is not only less contrasty, it has much more latitude than Kodachrome. If you wanted a particular effect with Kodachrome, exposure had to be absolutely accurate. There was no room for miscalculation or for error, and your judgment had to be perfect. With Kodachrome II, you have some leeway, and you can capture at least a passable picture even if your exposure is off by a stop or two. Unless you are quite critical, or comparison tests are run, the picture won't be a complete disappointment.

Tests made bracketing this film by half stops indicated that satisfactory transparencies could be made if the film were overexposed by as much as 1½ stops or underexposed by as much as two. The exposure taken as standard in these tests was a reflected-light reading with a Weston Master IV meter from an Eastman Kodak Neutral Grey Test Card (these cards are available at photographic stores), with the card facing the camera from subject position.

HOW CHARACTERISTICS CHANGE PICTURES

What do all these differences, in sharpness, in color, in speed, in contrast, in latitude, mean to you, the photographer? Let's take them up one by one.

The increased sharpness of Kodachrome II is much more important in movies than in stills. Kodachrome 35mm transparencies always looked absolutely and completely sharp. In that size, we simply can't *see any* improvement. Our eyes—and many lenses—are not that discerning. When testing the Kodachrome II against Kodachrome at *Modern Photography* magazine, we simultaneously pro-

Don't wait for the sun to shine to shoot landscapes. Exposure for this Puerto Rican beach scene on heavy overcast day was f/5.6 and 1/30 sec. with 50mm f/2 Summicron lens, Leica M3.

Try a wide aperture with longer-than-normal focal lengths for narrow depth of field. M. Meuer made this photograph with a Contarex camera, 85mm f/2 Zeiss Sonnar, Kodachrome II exposure 1/125 and f/2.8.

jected identical slides to the size of 4 x 6 feet with too matched projectors on matte screens. Examining tiny areas at a distance of a few inches from the screen, we could notice a difference. But at normal and closer-than-normal viewing distances, the superior sharpness of Kodachrome II was not apparent.

It's a different story in movies. Now, 16mm films rival 35mm in quality. And in the 8mm field, it's practically a revolution! The reasons for this are obvious. The 8mm movie frame is about 1/60 the size of the 35mm format, yet it is usually enlarged to about 2 x 3 feet on the screen. Compare this to the page size of most magazines, or to the conventional enlargement from 35mm—certainly no more than 11 x 14. True, the viewing distance is not the same, but even so the enlargement of 8mm film is extraordinary. If you are an 8mm movie maker, you should be able to notice an improvement in your efforts; but if you shoot 35mm or 828 size slides, either professionally for magazine reproduction or as an amateur aiming for projection or prints, you may not notice the difference in sharpness.

COLOR IS CLOSER TO NATURE

The improved color of Kodachrome II means that your transparencies will show more accurately what you actually saw when you took the picture. Roses will be redder, violets bluer, and people won't be purple when you photograph them in open shade. I've seen some portraits made on Kodachrome II Daylight Type in the shade of a building on a bright, sunny day. The subject was illuminated by skylight only, which actually is much bluer than the daylight mixture of direct sunlight and open sky for which all color films are balanced. After processing, the girl looked not blue at all, but had the normal, rosy skin "seen" when the photographer made the picture.

One of the main differences you will notice will be in the color of grass in your scenics or family photographs in the backyard. Greens are truer. With Kodachrome, they often deviated towards blue, particularly if the grass was in shade.

IT'S FASTER, YOU'RE FREER

The increased speed of Kodachrome II is particularly valuable for action or sports, or where greater depth of field is needed. Kodachrome II Type A, whose working index of about 50-60 (Eastman Kodak recommends 40, which we found best only in very contrasty light) makes available-light candids perfectly possible. Exposures were necessarily long with Kodachrome, and invariably required a tripod or other steady support. Correct exposure for a street scene could involve seconds or even minutes; with Kodachrome II, it's at least possible to use $1/30$ or $1/15$, if you can shoot wide open at $f/1.4$ or $f/2$.

The lowered contrast of the new Kodachrome II means that you will be able to photograph scenes, still lifes or people, with part of the subject brightly illuminated and other parts in shadow, and record detail in both. You'll no longer find part of your sitter's face a black blob if you're photographing in contrasty side light. And if you shoot against the light and expose for the shadows, you'll be able to hold detail in both the "correctly" exposed shadows and in the "overexposed" background. Suppose, for instance, you're making a portrait of a friend. You are outdoors on a bright, sunny day. First, you try posing your friend facing the sun. The result? He squints. You tell him to shut his eyes. You tell him to open them when you're ready to take the picture. He does, you shoot—and record a blink. You finally give up, have him turn around, and having decided you don't *care* if the background's burned out (not necessarily a bad technique, incidentally) you shoot away while he neither squints nor blinks. You're in for a delightful surprise when you see your processed film. There will be detail, and not so overexposed, in the background. And the color balance in the shaded face will look natural.

The added latitude of Kodachrome II is particularly valuable when working by available or tungsten light. It is really fairly difficult to expose incorrectly in bright sunlight. Most photographers can do fairly well just following the instructions packaged with the film. Exposure is another matter when you're working with available light.

Unlike film, the human eye adapts automatically for different types of lighting and unless one is extraordinarily observant and perceptive, he will not be able to tell without a great deal of experience exactly how light a room is. Obviously, if he has photographed there before, he will know on the basis of previous readings, or previous under- or overexposure. This difficulty is compounded by the fact that practically no indoor area—with the exception of indoor sports arenas or stages in theatres—is particularly evenly illuminated. I made a test, taking incident light readings in the living rooms of several friends. I found that the best of them showed a difference of three stops in various parts of the room where a possible subject might sit; the worst had a ten-stop difference in exposure.

Since Kodachrome II can be under- or overexposed somewhat without producing completely catastrophic results, and since it can handle extreme contrast with ease, seeing into the shadows while holding detail in the highlights, available light work at home or in the field will be much simpler than it was in the past. This is not, of course, a suggestion that you cease to be concerned with correct exposure. There is no substitute for it—and half stop differences in exposure will show up, even though slightly, on Kodachrome II. It is meant as reassurance that if your exposure is off your slides will not be completely ruined. If you are after candid pictures of people, where the main emphasis is *not* perfect color, contrast, or tone— as it would be if you were shooting, say, still lifes or landscapes— you can be a bit freer in concentrating on capturing spontaneity of gesture and expression. And you won't have to take out a meter every time your subject moves from one part of the room to another. You will be able to operate by guesswork, and won't have to interrupt the scene, increasing your subject's camera consciousness and decreasing your chances for better pictures.

Now that we've covered the important differences of Kodachrome II in general, let's go on and discuss specifically how to handle it in the field, in relation to the equipment you will use and the situations you will encounter.

CHAPTER TWO

Go Out and Shoot

The information in this chapter touches on material to be found in subsequent chapters: but here you'll find listed specific subjects and techniques for them which you may or may not want to follow up in their more detailed and technical form later in the book. The material here should be just enough to start you in the right direction with the subjects and situations covered, but since all items are cross referenced by page or chapter you will have no difficulty finding additional and more complete information connected with any phase of shooting which particularly interests you.

PEOPLE

Technically, the main thing to keep in mind when photographing people, indoors or out, in stills or movies, candidly or with a formal setup, is getting correct flesh tones. There's nothing more disconcerting than a green face, caused by the green reflected from nearby grass; or the blue, frozen-looking features caused by photographing in open shade, where light from a clear blue sky is the sole source; or a near-yellow countenance lit by the late afternoon sun, low in the sky. These effects are disconcerting, that is, if they were not what you saw and intended. There are warming and cooling filters discussed in Chapter 7 which can produce normal-looking flesh tones in any kind of lighting. For specific filters, I suggest you consult the tables on pages 71 and 74.

You will probably need filters, too, when shooting indoors, to keep flesh tones as well as the rest of the scene near normal. Here, the Kodak Wratten 81 and 82 series (table, page 71) will be of great help. Any imbalance between the color of your light source and that for which the film is balanced will be more noticeable in terms of people's faces than it will in the rest of the scene. There, in walls, furniture, lights, pictures or whatever, you have no easy frame of reference. Walls which are actually white could (if you didn't know better) be light blue or light yellow; but unless a person is suffering from chilblains or jaundice, you can never convince a viewer that he is light blue or light yellow. Remember, if your photographs of people do not have correct flesh tones, there can be only one reason for it: The illumination falling on your subject was not of the proper color. The simplest way to control this is to use one of these light-balancing filters: if faces seem too blue, use one of the yellowish, Kodak Wratten 81 series filters over your camera's lens to effectively lower the color temperature of the source. If faces seem too yellow, try one of the Wratten 82 series to raise effectively the color temperature of the source. Unless you own one of the color temperature meters (caution: most are meant to be used with tungsten light source only, not daylight) you will have to make a calculated guess. Or, before investing in the relatively expensive glass-mounted filters, try the plain gelatin filters, which are cheaper, to determine the exact warming or cooling effect you will need.

FILTERS FOR MOVIES

The need to keep flesh tones consistently near normal is considerably more important with movies than with stills. It's annoying to see your subject change color, seemingly right before your very eyes, as the scene shifts from open shade to bright sun; it's infuriating to have him transformed in different shots in the same situation. Decide in advance before filming which filters you will need to keep light balance the same in different lighting situations under which you will be working. The chart on page 69 should be of great help to you in noting the color temperature of various tungsten light sources, and for various kinds of outdoor lighting situations. Then, go to your shooting prepared. Unless your work is of

16

the most professional and critical nature (after all, no one is going to carp about small but obvious color shifts in shots of kids playing in the back yard) the decamired filter system described in detail on page 82 is probably the simplest solution for you. The table on page 83 gives decamired values for a number of different lighting situations, and should provide at least a valuable starting point, if not the final answer to all your problems. For critical professional work a color temperature meter will be an aid—but of course for the professional who is going to have prints made of his films, over-all color balance shifts can be made in printing. (More on this in chapter 9.)

PORTRAITURE THE EASY WAY

With the primary technical problem out of the way, let's go on to shooting techniques for people. I am of the opinion that unless one is an experienced professional, wise in the methods of putting people at their ease before the camera, the more candid the shooting technique the better. The most uninhibited and exuberant of personalties can somehow become self-conscious and constrained if he knows he is being photographed, or at least is made particularly aware of it. And one of the most trying and difficult fields of photography is that of portraiture.

One of the reasons, I am sure, is that many amateur photographers are not sufficiently relaxed themselves. Their tension communicates to their subjects, who, once tense, cannot easily be relaxed. So at first, try the candid approach.

Don't make elaborate lighting setups. With Kodachrome II, they aren't really necessary. The film is sufficiently fast and gives you enough leeway in exposure control, so that you can easily photograph by window light, by light in your subject's backyard, on his front porch, on the street in front of his house, or if you're shooting at night with a minimum of extra equipment (see chapters 5 and 6).

FILL THE FRAME

One of the biggest mistakes made by amateur photographers in general (I do not mean *advanced* amateurs. Advanced means by definition that one has outgrown this) is that they don't get close enough to people when they photograph them. Few things are more boring than full length photographs of people standing foursquare to the camera. Unless, of course, the photographs are either 100-year-old daguerreotypes or the subjects are relatives: in either of these cases, I will admit that this technique seems to have a certain primitive charm. Otherwise, get in close and try to fill the frame. Crop in on the head if you like. With the normal, 50mm lens on your 35mm rangefinder camera you can come within 3½ feet or so to make a head and shoulders portrait. (If you're nervous about distortion, or if your subject has a particularly large nose, have him turn his head ¼ away from the camera. But distortion probably won't be noticeable at this distance anyway.)

Portraits taken from four to six feet have an intimacy entirely lacking with long-lens pictures, and even if you do have an interchangeable-lens camera, don't neglect the normal focal length for pictures of people. I have never known whether to attribute this to the fact that many long-lens pictures of people are candid, semi-grab shots, taken at public events of public personalities, and hence there *was* no rapport between photographer and subject; or to the fact that if the shot was made from within a few feet the photographer couldn't have been too scared of his subject, thus lessening the chances for the subject to be too scared of him.

Most people are delighted to have their picture taken, unless, of course, they are shy or have some religious or superstitious reason which forbids the making of images. You are more likely to be greeted with pleasure and curiosity than with hostility. One peculiarity of this situation is that you are less likely to cause a stir if you work with a normal or wide-angle lens very close in to the people than if you try to stand back and shoot with a long lens from a distance. (This is assuming that the people don't mind being photographed. If they do, you have no alternative but to stay at a distance. Otherwise, you're liable to have your camera smashed.)

I have photographed at places like parties, markets, carnivals, on the street, in parks, and have found that when I'm working within two feet of my subject with a 28mm lens on a 35mm camera, I'm less likely to cause a stir than if I'm 25 ft. away with a 200mm. Probably, it's just that if you are that close to him, it doesn't occur to the ordinary, non-photographer subject that you might actually be photographing him—it must be that other fellow ten feet behind.

About lighting for people: there actually are no rules. But do keep in mind that both the quality of light and its color do affect the mood of the picture. You probably wouldn't want to use strong, contrasty sidelight for a photograph of a delicate, golden-haired little girl; but then again, you might. Here, it's a matter of taste and of what you have to say. In general, hazy or overcast weather is excellent for outdoor portraits; try bounce light if you're shooting indoors (see page 64).

PROPS

Again, there are no rules about props except that they should be appropriate to the subject. There are several ways of using props with people. One, the environmental prop, suggests something specific about the sitter's profession or personality. The best-known, and probably most expert, practitioner of this approach to portraiture is Arnold Newman, who places his subjects in situations suggestive of their work. Thus, a theatre critic is photographed in an empty theatre; with the vacant seats used as an element in the overall design; a pianist is photographed seated at the piano, with the shape of the instrument the dominant compositional element, the artist himself posed so as to seem almost a part of it.

The other reason for using props—equally legitimate—is to give your subject something to do. You may simply prefer not to take a straight portrait: your subject may be tense and camera-shy; you may be shooting for a variety of expressions and compositions; if the subject is a child, he may lose interest without some prop—a toy, book, or pet—practically before you've begun to photograph him. While the prop here is definitely secondary to the subject, you must exercise caution in choosing it. Many a portrait which would otherwise be acceptable has been ruined by tasteless or thoughtless selection of props. The viewer of a picture should never ask himself "What is that person doing with that prop?" If the question is asked, the prop is unsuitable.

CHILDREN

If props may often be desirable for pictures of adults, they are practically mandatory for children. Some children are perfectly natural before the camera; others consistently eye it frozen-faced, with a glassy stare, or, at the opposite extreme, with simple minded grins or facial contortions hopefully not representative of their usual appearance. If they can be involved in some natural activity—playing in a sandpile, throwing a ball, having a tea party for dolls, examining a flower—you'll probably turn up a considerably better set of photographs than if you try to pose them.

ANIMALS

If the animal you are photographing is a well-trained pet your job is half over. If not, try bribing him to stay put and look interested with small bits of food. Photograph active pets in action. Try panning (see below) as a dog races to retrieve a stick (you'll need an assistant to throw it) or use electronic flash to stop the motion of a cat leaping after a piece of string. Special pets — birds, fish, lions, snails, etc. — require special approaches; two of the most useful are close-up (Chapter 7) and electronic flash (Chapter 6). If yours is a furry pet, use cross light to bring out texture; if it's wild fauna you're after, use a long lens, walk with stealth, build a blind, and in general practice the techniques of the hunter. Backgrounds for animals as for people should be simple.

KNOW YOUR CAMERA

If you are taking pictures of buildings, of landscapes, of flowers, you have some time to decide on composition, and set the camera's controls carefully. Your subject isn't going to change much in a matter of seconds. But split-second timing is all-important if your subjects are human. I cannot overemphasize the importance of being thoroughly familiar with your camera's controls if you are interested in photographing people. Since at times you will have to work very fast—or at least, you *should* work very fast—you must be able to change shutter speed, aperture, and focus almost unconsciously. Practice shooting fast without film in the camera. And practice just focusing, shooting and advancing the film.

ACTION

The subjects you may want to shoot in action are probably countless. Children, pets, sports events, to mention just a few of the more obvious. We aren't going to set up rules; *i.e.*, precisely what shutter speed you need to stop the motion of an object moving at a speed of 40mph parallel to the camera at a distance of 25 feet. In general action is stopped *best* when the subject is moving directly toward or away from the camera; it is stopped *less* when the subject is moving at an angle to the camera; it is stopped *least* when the subject is moving directly across the field of view. Here are two other basic points to keep in mind when photographing fast action with still cameras:

1. *Camera-to-subject distance* is a factor affecting shutter speed needed to stop action. If a person walks past a camera at a distance of five feet, the image will be much more blurred than if the person passed at 25 ft. at the same rate of speed and you used the same lens opening and shutter speed for both. If you want to stop action, you are safest using a fairly fast speed—upwards of 1/125 sec.— and the additional speed of Kodachrome II enables you to do this easily in most outdoor lighting situations. And, believe it or not, stopping action can be a terrific problem when shooting close-ups. An ant plodding across a leaf at a distance of 3 inches from the camera's lens will register just as much blur at 1/25 sec. as a baseball player dashing for first base at a distance of 200 yards.

2. *Lens focal length* should also be considered when you set the shutter speed you will need to stop action. A charging football player will seem much more blurred if photographed from 100 feet with a 200mm lens than with a 50mm using the same shutter speed.

In movies, of course, unless you have a variable shutter, you cannot control speed.

A number of different kinds of action have what is called a peak, or moment when the action comes completely or nearly to a stop and reverses its direction. A child jumping or swinging, a pole vaulter at the top of his jump, are obvious examples. If you can sharpen your sense of timing and make your exposure at precisely the peak of action, you can use a considerably slower shutter speed

21

and produce sharper pictures than if you shoot a moment sooner or later.

ZONE FOCUS

One of the most useful techniques for action is zone focus. Look at the lens mount of your camera. The exact appearance of depth-of-field markings for use with the zone focus technique varies from lens to lens, but on all lenses you will see two sets of identical numbers, one on each side of the distance setting indicator. The distance in depth which will be in focus at any given aperture for any distance setting that falls between the identical numbers which are the same as the f/number you are using (*i.e.*, the numbers on the depth of field scale—2, 2.8, 4, 5.6, etc., actually represent the f/numbers $f/2$, $f/2.8$, $f/4$, $f/5.6$, etc.) Obviously, the smaller the aperture (bigger f/number), the greater the depth of field. To use the zone focus technique for action, simply estimate the near and far distances between which the action will take place or measure them with your camera's rangefinder, and fit these distances between the smallest possible identical set of f/numbers on the depth-of-field-scale by adjusting lens focus. For example, if you are photographing a football game with a 50mm lens on a 35mm camera and want to photograph action between 15 and 50 feet from your vantage point, fit the 15 and 50 foot distance markings on the lens between the smallest possible set of identical f/numbers on the mount, which, in this case, would be 5.6. $F/5.6$ is the largest aperture you can use and keep everything between 15 and 50 feet in sharp focus. Depth of field is also a particularly important consideration when doing close-ups, and we will discuss it in more detail in Chapter 8.

If you are shooting indoors and have complete control of the situation, you can—and should—try electronic flash. The short duration of flash (1/500 to 1/2000 sec. for most amateur units) will stop any but the most violent action. Speedlights are particularly useful for close-up, too (see Chapter 8).

While Kodachrome II is a sufficiently fast film to allow you to stop most action, there will be times when you won't want to. Try panning—moving the camera with the moving subject during the exposure—which when successful keeps the subject sharp but blurs the background. Track the subject with the camera to your eye for a split second before shooting and keep the subject centered in the viewfinder. Try moving your whole upper body to insure a smooth pan (unless, of course, your camera is on a tripod, most of which have heads specially meant for panning, which is a standard movie technique) rather than just the shoulders.

LANDSCAPES

For clear, accurate reproduction of all the colors found in nature, Kodachrome II is unsurpassed. The greatest difference you will notice when using it outdoors is in its rendition of greens, which contain no hint of the bluish cast to which we are accustomed with Kodachrome, particularly when exposed in open shade.

If you have been using a Kodak Skylight Filter for all of your outdoor shooting, I suggest that you try photographing without it with Kodachrome II. Some photographers have found that this filter "warms up" Kodachrome II too much; however, since color balance is a matter of taste, try shooting several scenes with and without the filter. Then you can decide which you prefer.

With landscapes, and, actually, with any subject, when you are using Kodachrome II, I suggest that you adjust the exposure index according to the light quality. This is discussed in detail later in the book, but, briefly: if the light is contrasty, stick to the manufacturer's recommended E.I. 25; if it is very flat, use E.I. 40 for the most rich saturated color.

While you may not want to use the Kodak Skylight Filter for close and middle-distance work with nature subjects, it will still probably be desirable when you are photographing distant subjects with long focal length lenses. Here, you will need to cut through atmospheric haze and eliminate ultraviolet if you are even to get an image of your subject.

A word about lighting conditions for landscapes. Don't wait for the sun to shine, unless you are interested in purely post card views. And, in my opinion, if you *are* interested in post card views, you'd be better off buying post cards or sets of travel slides of the area. Shoot your Kodachrome II in the fog, in rainstorms, when the sky is overcast, before 9 A.M. and after 3 P.M.; if you've been confining your shooting to bright midday sun, you'll be amazed and delighted by the beauty of the results. Side lighting, early or late in the day, is particularly useful in revealing texture.

It's a good idea when shooting landscapes to try to find a suitable frame. There are, of course, exceptions to this rule—but in general more landscapes suffer from lack of any dominant foreground interest than from its inclusion.

For more detailed information on shooting landscapes, see Chapter 4. Chapter 7, on Filters, also contains a great deal of helpful information, particularly on the polarizing filter and its use.

CLOSE IN ON NATURE

The advice to come in close to people can be applied equally to a number of subjects in nature. While extreme close-ups—closer than the focusing ability of your camera's lens—are covered in detail in Chapter 8, you can make extremely exciting photographs within the normal focusing range. Try wide apertures to throw backgrounds out of focus—or set focus at a distance but include out-of-focus foreground objects, such as leaves, in the frame.

CHECK THESE BEFORE YOU SHOOT

Here are some simple technical points to keep in mind. Check this list off before you actually load your camera, and start to shoot. For 35mm and 828:

1. Watch the light. Never load or unload your camera in bright sun. If possible, change films indoors, or in the shade of a building or tree. If necessary, a coat held over your head while your back is turned to the sun can provide sufficient shade.

2. Check to be certain that film is threaded and moving properly before you shut the camera back. Load according to

camera manufacturer's instructions. On 35mm cameras, turn rewind back gently until it will move no further (be careful not to cinch film tightly or you will scratch it). Then, when you click off the first two or three frames necessary before your first exposure, you will be able to see the rewind knob turn as you advance the film.

3. With flash, check batteries before shooting. Batteries for flash are exhausted in a matter of months even if they are not used. Some brands have expiration date marked on them.

4. Remove lens cap. It seems ridiculous, but this is still one of the greatest causes of ruined pictures.

5. When you have finished shooting, rewind 35mm film completely back into the cassette to avoid confusing exposed with unexposed film.

For movie camera users:

1. Do not load camera in bright light. Movie film, particularly roll film, can easily be light struck if you load your camera in sunlight. If possible, load and change films indoors in subdued light. If you must change film outdoors, find a shaded spot or cover your head and shoulders with a coat, keeping your back to the sun.

2. With roll film: keep the paper band to put around the exposed film. Keep the light-colored side of the film toward the lens when you thread the camera.

3. With magazines: keep magazines in their shipping cartons when they are not actually in the camera. Handle them carefully, since if they are bent they will not operate properly. Do not remove the tape from the magazine. If you do, you risk light striking the film.

4. When loading a 16mm magazine, be certain that the pin on the magazine top is at the forward end of the slot and that it fits in the notch in the camera. The shutter on the front of 16mm magazines should be completely closed. If it isn't, turn pin on magazine front to close.

5. 8mm magazine must be properly inserted in the camera. To start, insert magazine first side up as marked, then set footage indicator. When entire 25 ft. of film is exposed, remove magazine, turn, and insert as marked 2nd side up, and proceed to expose remaining 25 ft.

6. Do not reseal the foil packing of magazines. Simply place the magazine in its yellow carton for processing. With rolls, replace the paper band and return film to original can.

MOST COMMON CAUSES FOR BAD PICTURES

Here's another check list—this one need be consulted only if you're disappointed after receiving your Kodachrome II back from the processor. You can easily scan it to pick out your particular trouble, and its possible cause and solution.

Pictures too dark or too light: If you've followed the exposure instructions packaged with the film or your meter, the trouble may be with your camera's shutter or with the meter. Be certain that you had the exposure index set correctly on the meter, E.I. 25 to 40 for Kodachrome II Daylight Type, E.I. 40 to 64 for Type A, depending on lighting contrast. If E.I. setting was correct, check meter against one known to be accurate, and have camera shutter checked by a repairman.

No image on film: There are a number of possible reasons. The film may not have gone through the camera due to improper loading. Make certain that the film is attached to the take-up spool and moving over the sprockets (with 35mm) before closing the camera. Follow your camera manufacturer's instructions for loading. Another possible reason for completely black film is not removing the lens cap.

A third is failure of flash synchronization. Check your camera manufacturer's instruction booklet to be certain that you are using flash bulbs or electronic flash at the right speeds. Check flash batteries before shooting flash pictures, since they can be exhausted even if they haven't been used. Or, the sync can be off in the camera itself. If you are certain that you used the correct shutter speed and that the batteries of your flash unit are not exhausted, have your camera's sync checked by a reliable repairman.

Blurred or fuzzy pictures: If the main subject only is blurred, the shutter speed was too slow for the rate of action. Use a higher speed or try panning the camera with action. If the whole picture is blurred, the camera was probably moved during exposure. Squeeze shutter release gently; concentrate on holding still while making an exposure. Be certain camera is not set on time or bulb unless you are intentionally making a long exposure with a tripod. If the subject is fuzzy, the focus was not set or judged accurately. Check depth-of-field on lens mount or separate depth-of-field scale. If lens is fixed focus, camera was probably too close to subject. See Chapter 8 for use of close-up lenses with fixed focus movie cameras. If rangefinder camera, check rangefinder if you are certain that focus was originally set accurately. If single-lens-reflex, have mirror alignment checked.

Right density, wrong color: If the color is deep red, green, orange, etc., the probable cause is that you left a filter meant for black-and-white on the camera by accident. If the pictures are bluish, you may have exposed Kodachrome II Type A by daylight illumination; if reddish, you may have used Kodachrome II Daylight Type by tungsten light, or shot too early or late in the day for "natural" color rendition. See Chapter 7 on filters for information on how to correct. If your slides or movie footage is greenish, reddish, or washed out and mottled, it may have been outdated (watch the expiration date on the film package) or subjected to high humidity and/or heat before processing. Keep film in package until ready to use, have it processed promptly after exposure.

Fog, light or dark streaks: Camera may leak light; back may have come open in the middle of a roll; light source (particularly likely if you were shooting backlight) may have been hitting lens, causing reflections. Dark spots or lines probably caused by dust or torn bits of film casting shadows in camera. Keep interior of camera clean with blower, camel's hair brush. Dark, ragged looking edge at top or bottom of projected movie frame caused by film emulsion or dirt lodged in film gate of projector or camera. Check manufacturer's instructions for cleaning.

Vibration of projected movies: Camera or projector not threaded properly, or out of adjustment. Check instruction booklet.

CHAPTER THREE

Exposure

While the increased latitude of Kodachrome II will help to excuse
the most flagrant of exposure errors, this is no excuse for making
them. In order to understand how exposure really affects Kodachrome
II—and how exposure can work for you—I suggest that you make
a test, using one roll of Kodachrome II. Choose a subject illuminated
by direct sunlight. It can be a portrait, a scenic or a close-up, but
it should include both sunlit and shaded areas. Then take a meter
reading, and set your aperture at $f/5.6$ and your shutter speed as
indicated by the meter. Now, run through the complete gamut of
exposures from $f/2$ to $f/16$ in half stops (or from $f/3.5$ to $f/22$, or
however your camera is marked); *i.e.* shoot at $f/2$, advance the film,
shoot at $f/2.2$, advance, at $f/2.8$, advance, at $f/3.5$, advance, etc. You
will have a total of 13 exposures. When your film is returned from
the processor, line these slides up in sequence on the light box, and
mark the f/number at which each was shot on the mount.

The slide shot at $f/5.6$ is that exposed normally; $f/2$ is three stops
overexposed, $f/16$ is three stops underexposed. You may very well
find that you prefer one of the slides over- or underexposed to the
"normal" $f/5.6$ exposure. If so, decide whether you feel this way
because of the specific subject—*i.e.*, you prefer a light, high key
overexposure, or the drama, saturated color, and density of an
underexposure because it is more suitable to your subject; or if
you prefer this under- or overexposure for all your color work. If so,
you can expose consistently in this fashion.

29

Without such a basis for comparison, it is impossible to decide how you should expose your Kodachrome II. I would say from my experience in viewing slides at *Modern Photography* that most photographers' difficulty does not stem from sloppy and erratic exposure techniques which produce different slide densities without relation to subject; most of the unsolicited material which we receive is surprisingly consistent in exposure. But it may be over- or underexposed according to any standard which might be set up. If these photographers had ever performed such a test they would have considerably more choice; it might occur to them that different subjects probably call for different exposure approaches in color; and most important, that even a ½ stop difference is certainly a noticeable one. You will see from your experiments with Kodachrome II that while you have some image all the way through the full range of stops from $f/2$ to $f/16$ (this is not true with Kodachrome) and that the image is acceptable through a three or four stop range, the effect will vary and the color will vary noticeably even between half stop exposure differences.

There are a number of excellent exposure meters on the market, ranging in price from $160 for the super-sensitive spot-reading SEI, made in Great Britain, to $20-$35 for the Weston, the General Electric, and the Norwood Director. Other good meters are marketed by Agfa, Bewi, Gossen, Sekonic, Walz, Sixtomat and by camera manufacturers such as E. Leitz and Nikon. If you are shooting movies you will find a meter which gives apertures directly for fps (frames per second) most convenient. For practical purposes, there are basically two types of meters. Reflected light meters, such as the Weston and the General Electric, read the light reflected back into the camera from the subject, and if used close up on specific parts of the subject, take into account the differences in reflectance from different parts; *i.e.*, a black jacket may read 25, while the face will meter about 600 or 800 in bright sunlight.

The incident reading meters, such as the Norwood Director, are for reading the light falling onto the subject. The correct technique for using them is to hold them at subject position with the cone aimed directly at the camera.

The following meters are fairly specialized and fairly expensive. Each of them, however, is an extremely useful instrument for making spot readings of a distant subject and/or because of its extremely high sensitivity, as indicated.

Elwood Foto-Meter Model Z-4 can be set for exposure indexes from .2-6400, covers shutter speeds from 8 to 1/1000 sec., apertures from *f*/1 to *f*/45. This highly sensitive spot-reading reflected light meter reads an angle of 2 degrees, is powered by mercury batteries, indicates LVS and Polaroid numbers, 16, 32, 64 frames per second. Approximate price, $90, case $15.

Elwood Foto-Meter Model 92 can be set for exposure indexes from 1 to 16,000, covers shutter speeds from 30 to 1/2000 sec., apertures from *f*/1 to *f*/45. This spot-reading reflected light meter is similar to Z-4 above, but reads a 4 degree angle of light. Approximate price $47.50 with case.

Gossen Lunasix can be set for exposure indexes from 6 to 12,000, covers shutter speeds from eight hours to 1/4000 sec., apertures from *f*/1 to *f*/90. This reflected or incident meter is super-sensitive, reads in LVS, has cadmium sulfide cell, mercury battery. Approximate price, $63 with case and strap.

Honeywell Pentax 3°/21° con be set for exposure indexes from 3 to 6400, covers shutter speeds from 4 to 1/4000 sec., apertures from *f*/1 to *f*/45. This spot-reading reflected light meter reads a 3 degree angle of light, uses cadmium sulfide cell, 2 mercury batteries. Approximate price $79.50 with batteries, case.

S.E.I. Photometer can be set for exposure indexes from 1 to 1000, covers speeds from 2 hours 47 min. to 1/500,000 sec., apertures from *f*/1 to *f*/32. This reflected optical spot comparison meter reads a ½ degree angle of light, uses one D cell battery, may be used as a densitometer. Approximate price, $170 with case.

Spectra Combi 500 Professional can be set for exposure indexes from .1 to 32,000, covers shutter speeds from 8 hours to 1/4000 sec., apertures from *f*/.5 to *f*/45. This incident meter has a reflected light attachment, 13 individual direct reading scales for 1/50 sec., covers 8, 16, 32, and 64 frames per second, has battery powered cadmium sulfide and selenium cells. Approximate price, $127.50 with incident attachment, booster.

There are two special methods for using reflected meters which you may find a help, particularly when photographing subjects which are at a distance. One is to take a reading from the palm of your hand and give one stop less exposure than indicated. The other, called the substitute method, is to select an object close to your position which seems to be of approximately the same color and tone as the distant subject you are photographing and take a reading from it.

You must remember, whether your meter is the reflected or incident type, that the readings you take with it can be used only as a starting point (many of each variety, incidentally, have accessories which convert them to make readings using the other technique). You have to use your head. Take into account the darkness, lightness, the contrast within the scene and the lighting. If the subject is dark, open up ½ to 1 stop from the reading indicated by an incident meter; if the subject is very light and you are using an incident meter, close down ½ to 1 stop for a transparency of "normal" density. I emphasize this, because you very well may not want a transparency of normal density, or at least you shouldn't in every situation. This control over density is one of the few you have when working with a reversal transparency film such as Kodachrome II. You don't have the processing controls that you have with black-and-white film and with some of the other reversal color materials mentioned in the first chapter.

With black-and-white film, the rule is expose for the shadows, develop for the highlights. Since you cannot change development for Kodachrome II or for Kodachrome, exposure is usually based on a highlight reading. This does not mean that you should aim your reflected light meter at the highest tone in the subject and expose as indicated. The arrow on the Weston dial, the pointer on the GE, are meant to indicate a middle density reading, a tone actually equivalent to that of an Eastman Kodak 18% reflectance grey card, or the same as the average reading indicated by an incident meter. With a reflected light meter, take a reading from a middle tone; or if you read from the flesh tones, give one stop more exposure than indicated, since you are actually reading from one of the lightest parts of the subject. If the face tones are rendered as a middle tone, as they will be if you expose as indicated by the arrow or pointer, the transparency will probably be darker than you want it.

With Kodachrome II, lighting contrast becomes a very important factor governing exposure. If the lighting is very flat, as on an overcast day, all differences in contrast depend on tones within the subject. If you expose as indicated by an incident light reading, or follow your usual reflected light technique, your resulting transparencies will probably look overexposed, and even though highlights will retain detail, there won't be any tones dark enough to give contrast and snap to the picture. In such situations, I suggest either underexposing by half a stop or changing the recommended E.I. to 40.

ANOTHER METHOD: CHANGE E.I.

What is E.I.? This abbreviation stands for exposure index, a number assigned by the manufacturer to indicate the speed of his film. Photographers working in black-and-white are accustomed to altering the recommended E.I. of their films, and changing development to get excellent results with either higher or lower ratings. With Kodachrome II, possibilities for changing E.I. and compensating with development do not exist as with some other color films, as discussed in Chapter 1.

The recommended E.I. is a practical working number arrived at by purely subjective visual tests. The E.I. represents no more or less than the speed rating which under average lighting conditions should produce best results. If you keep this in mind, you can see how simple it is to change it for different lighting conditions rather than remembering to under- or overexpose and leave it constant.

In very flat light you will need to "underexpose" to produce a transparency which is of acceptable density. You can, just as simply, adjust the exposure index of Kodachrome II Daylight Type and shoot at approximately E.I. 40. The reverse is true as well; if the lighting is extremely contrasty and you want to record shadow detail, set the exposure index lower than you would for normal lighting conditions, at about E.I. 25. The lighting contrast itself will provide all the punch you need, and the same subject photographed in this type of lighting will not seem overexposed as it would in the previously discussed lighting situation. This technique was not applicable to Kodachrome film, since its greater contrast and narrower latitude made it necessary always to expose for the highlights, if you were working for a normal transparency.

Understanding E.I., and using it in this way, is important in all camera work; but it becomes more important if you work with a camera having the LV system and/or a coupled meter, and all-important if you work with one of the new electric-eye cameras. First, let's discuss the LV system and how it works.

EVS stands for Exposure Value System, LVS for Light Value System. The numbers are the same. EVS-LVS numbers run from 1 to 16 or 20, and represent different levels of illumination. In addition to the regular numbers appearing on many meters manufactured since 1957, EVS numbers also appear. On a bright sunny day, the EV will be about 16. If you work with a camera having this system, you set the film speed, then set the EVS dial to, say, 16. As you move the EVS dial, the shutter or aperture dial (which depends on your specific camera) will move with it. Suppose your first picture is of a child, and you want to take a close-up portrait. Here, you are more concerned with getting sufficient depth of field, so you want to shoot at $f/11$. Simply turn the aperture dial to $f/11$, and the shutter speed coupled to it will turn simultaneously to 1/60. Your next shot, in the same lighting situation, is of a fast-moving ball game, the players 30 feet or so from the camera. Now, you need a faster speed to stop action. Turn the shutter speed indicator to 1/250, and aperture will move with it to $f/5.6$. The lighting for both pictures is the same, and the EV system has given you the correct f/stop and shutter speed combination to produce the best density in your final transparency. Suppose, however, that the lighting situation is extremely flat and you will want to "underexpose." It's difficult to think of shooting ½ or 1 stop under with a system such as LVS. (You can, of course, lower the EVS number by ½ or 1.) It is considerably more confusing than approaching it the other way around, in terms of adjusting your original E.I. film speed rating, which you can do easily with any camera.

If it is difficult to think in terms of under- and overexposure with LVS cameras and cameras with meters coupled to aperture or shutter speed, it is almost impossible with the new electric-eye still and movie cameras. When set on automatic, some of these cameras give no indication of what aperture or shutter speed you are using, to say nothing of any choice about the particular combination you want. If you are to produce correctly exposed transparencies in all kinds of lighting with these cameras, you must learn to assess the lighting contrast and adjust E.I. accordingly, since there is absolutely no possibility of even thinking in terms of specific f/numbers or shutter speeds.

I suggest that you run a set of experiments with these cameras, making a number of pictures of the same subject in the same lighting, and changing the exposure index setting on the camera between exposures. Start at the lowest setting, probably E.I. 8 or 10; then try 15, 20, 25, 30, 40, 60, and 100 with Kodachrome II. You will be amazed at the different effects you get, and more amazed that so many of them are acceptable! Try this with several different subject-lighting situations, and be certain to mark the E.I. you used on the slide mount when the slides are returned from the processor (since Kodachrome II transparencies are always numbered and packed in sequence, and since the slides will become progressively darker, this is no problem). Then, when you have compiled a reference series covering the different kinds of subject-lighting situations you will probably encounter, sit down and make a list of the subject-lighting situations. Next to each mark the E.I. which gave you the best results. You will probably find that an E.I. of 25 for Kodachrome II Daylight Type was best when shooting a portrait with very contrasty cross lighting; you may find, if you shot a piece of light driftwood on a white sand beach in very flat lighting, that an E.I. of 40 or even 50 gives you the best results.

Which E.I. is best for any situation will, of course, depend to some degree on your own taste: some photographers prefer transparencies which are fairly dense and have rich, saturated colors; others like lighter, more transparent hues. The best E.I. will also, of course, depend on the specific minor differences in transmission between any two lenses of the same type. This is true for all cameras, not just for those operating by the electric-eye system.

Until now, I have been concerned with indicating how to achieve normal exposure for any given situation. Until you know how to do this, it isn't possible for you to really be able to use exposure creatively, to under- or overexpose for special effects.

In movie work, of course, both 8 and 16mm, you will probably not want to use under- or overexposure as creative techniques. There, your main problem is to keep exposure as consistent as possible since you will be putting together pictures shot at different times in different situations. If you aren't extremely careful in choosing your situations as well as in trying whenever possible to control lighting contrast, you will never be able to match effectively different batches of footage and put them together into a cohesive whole. If, of course, your only interest in movie making is keeping a record of your growing children or of family functions, such considerations are not so important, since you are not producing a unit of film which should hold together technically and artistically.

With movies, incidentally, you only have to worry about aperture settings, since shutter speed is determined by the number of frames per second. Sixteen is the usual number for amateur movie makers, unless you plan to add a sound track, in which case you will be shooting at 24 fps. At 16 fps the shutter speed is about 1/30, at 24 fps, about 1/50 sec. Check the exact shutter speed for your camera at a given fps in the manufacturer's instruction booklet. Many meters have FPS markings on their dial, and give direct readings in f/stops for the given fps. If your meter does not have markings for fps, just read the speed opposite the 1/30 sec. if you are shooting at 16, or opposite 1/50 if you are shooting at 24 fps. As you increase fps for slow-motion work to 32 or 64, shutter speeds increase, usually to 1/80 and 1/125 sec. If you are shooting slow motion, read the apertures falling opposite 1/80 or 1/125 on the dial. Information on actual shutter speeds at different numbers of frames per second is supplied with every movie camera, and there are differences from camera to camera.

CHAPTER FOUR

Outdoors From Dawn to Dusk

The sun is a powerful light source. And the combination of a number of factors—different times of day, atmospheric conditions, time of year, lighting angle, and the color of objects located near the subject—produce an infinite variety of different types of illumination, all called sunlight.

Remember that all color films are built to produce natural-looking color with one light source and one only. For this reason, there are different films for daylight, for flash, for flood and for the standard photographic lamps. Kodachrome II Daylight Type, like most other daylight type color films, is balanced to produce normal colors only when exposed by one of the different types of light produced by the sun; loosely that typical of a clear day between 9 A.M. and 3 P.M.

Probably the most important variable in sunlight to the color photographer is the actual color of the light which reaches his subjects. In order to better understand the variations in the color of light from the sun, it is necessary to consider the nature of light. Light is that form of radiant energy which affects our sense of sight. Different colors of light represent different wave lengths: the longest wave lengths are red; the shortest, violet. When any substance is heated to incandescence, the wave length of the light it emits depends almost entirely on the temperature to which it is heated. Therefore, it is possible to indicate the color of illumination by the temperature to which a substance would have to be heated to produce light of

WHITE LIGHT, OR THE VISIBLE SPECTRUM

(In Millimicrons)

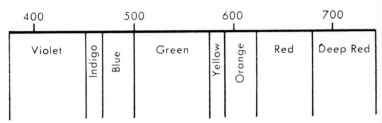

From "Filter Guide" by Norman Rothschild and Cora Wright, published by Amphoto.

THE ELECTRO-MAGNETIC SPECTRUM

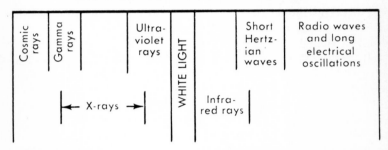

From "Filter Guide" by Norman Rothschild and Cora Wright, published by Amphoto.

the same color, or wave length. Color temperature is indicated in degrees Kelvin, which is numerically equal to degrees Centigrade plus 273. Color temperature, (not accurately, but for practical purposes) can be used to indicate the color of many kinds of light, even those which have not been produced by heat, such as the color of the light reflected from the sky or from a red brick wall, or from a green lawn.

The color temperature of daylight depends on all of the factors mentioned above. Let's take them one by one.

1) Time of year. On an average, the color temperature of direct sunlight alone, between the hours of 9 A.M. and 3 P.M. will vary with the season from about 5800K to 5450K. Differences in the angle at which the sun hits the earth, differences in distance from the sun to the location, differences in the amount of atmosphere which the sunlight must penetrate account for this.

2) Time of day. On a single sunny summer day, color temperature may range from 11,000 just before dawn, when all the illumination is coming from a clear blue sky, to 5200K at 8 A.M., to 5800K at noon, and back down to about 5000K just before sunset. How, you ask, can the range be so great? Just before dawn, all light reaching the subject will be from the sky. Light reflected from the sky alone is intensely blue, as indicated by the extraordinarily high color temperature. Once the sun is over the horizon, color temperature shifts abruptly, and will be considerably lower than at midday. This is because molecules and dust particles in the air scatter the shorter blue wave lengths, but allow the longer, red wave lengths to pass through the atmosphere and reach the subject. As the sun rises, its light passes through less atmosphere; hence more of the shorter, blue wave lengths reach the subject and the color temperature of the light is higher. The process is reversed as the sun sets, until just after sunset, color temperature of the illumination is again extremely high.

3) Atmospheric conditions. On a clear and cloudless day, skylight makes up about 20% of the total illumination; direct sunlight the rest. Clouds cut down much more proportionally on direct sunlight than on skylight; hence as the weather becomes more cloudy, color temperature of illumination rises somewhat. Skylight, however, is blue by reflection of the short blue waves. Since this blue color, if completely blanketed by clouds, is cut out, color temperature will drop.

4) Lighting angle. As indicated, the color of the illumination changes with time of day, as the sun is directly overhead, and as it goes down towards the horizon. Also, at any given time of day, as camera angle changes in relation to light, the color temperature of the light illuminating your subject will change. Try the following. Make a portrait outdoors, at about 2 or 3 P.M. First, have your subject turn around, with his back directly to the sun. Move around the subject, and have him turn to face you, take another meter reading (with a reflected meter, take a close-up reading from the face) and make another exposure. When you compare the processed transparencies, you will be able to see a difference in the flesh tones. The tones in the direct sun portrait will be much warmer; here, the face was illuminated by the usual combination of direct sunlight and skylight, for which the film is balanced; in the backlit portrait skylight, with its notably higher color temperature, was the source of illumination and more blue light was reflected from the face back into the camera.

5) Color of nearby objects. The degree to which colored objects located near your subject will affect its color depends on what proportion of the total illumination they account for. If your subject is next to a brilliant green wall, and if the light source is aimed at this wall, the side of the subject next to the wall will be greenish. Fine, if you like green shadows, but . . .

CONSIDER ITS QUALITY

Color is not the only attribute of sunlight which must be considered by the color photographer. Another important aspect of the light is its quality, and the relatively of the quality of illumination to its mood. Time of day and weather conditions are the two main factors which determine the quality of light.

The contrasty side light produced when the sun is near the horizon and barely skimming over the landscape is the most dramatic of the day. It casts harsh shadows, revealing texture, creating brilliant

40

contrasts. There are few subjects which are best illuminated by high, overhead noontime light, and I feel that most photographers would be better off if they kept their cameras in their gadget bags between 10 A.M. and 2 P.M.—the hours often recommended for picture taking, and confined their shooting to earlier and later hours, as much because of the more dramatic lighting quality as because of the unusual color effects which we discussed earlier.

Stop and think for a moment. If you were taking a picture indoors —a portrait, a still life, an action shot—and you could use only one point source for illumination, where would you place it in relation to your subject? Directly overhead? Most unlikely. You might place it directly behind your subject for backlight; you could have it slightly above and to one side; you might have it to one side, with a reflector close to your subject on the other side casting light back into the shadows. But certainly, not overhead. At least not for any subjects I know of. The situation with the sun is actually identical. It is a single point light source, with the added advantage of a built-in canopy, the sky, reflecting some illumination back, in and around to the other sides of the subject. But, remember, a point source casting light in all directions in a white-walled room with a white ceiling, would approximate the bright-sun-outdoors situation. The difference is an intensity of illumination, not in its quality or direction. In effect, the whole outdoors is a studio; the sun, a single lamp over which you have no control. For this reason you must train yourself to watch the sun, and become sensitive to its quality. When working indoors, you can move lights, use diffusing disks, build tents, use walls as reflectors, etc. Out of doors, you are at the mercy of Mother Nature, and you should be sensitive to all of her moods.

LIGHTING FOR MOOD

Actually, mood in color is created both by atmospheric conditions and by time of day. All too often amateur photographers wait until the sun shines to unlimber their cameras, go out and shoot. If confining your picture-taking to the hours between 10 and 2 is unfortunate, ignoring days ranging from slightly overcast to foggy, throwing in thunderstorms and blizzards for good measure, is downright tragic. Some of the most beautiful color photographs I have ever seen have been made on foggy days; some of the most dramatic winter shots during heavy snow storms. It's close to fact that if the weather is nice to be out in, it's probably not so great for picture taking, and the reverse. On slightly overcast days, the light takes on a luminous quality; and this quality (as well as the unusual color discussed above) is eminently capturable on Kodachrome II.

Overcast, almost foggy weather is ideal for portraiture, and for many kinds of nature close-ups (see Chapter 8). Slightly hazy days are excellent for just about everything, since they cut down on lighting contrast. Further, hazy or overcast weather opens up the full day to picture taking—for, as I said, it seems to me that the conventional hours for shooting when the sun is out rarely produce much more than conventional pictures.

Rainy or snowy weather is excellent for many daytime pictures, but it also opens up tremendous possibilities for night-time shooting. Lights from street lamps, from windows, or for that matter, from the moon (if you're interested in really long exposures), are reflected and the landscape or cityscape is much more brightly illuminated by this reflected light than in dry, summer weather. Remember, most buildings, streets, etc., are dark, as are grass and trees, and reflect little of the available illumination.

These special lighting conditions must be dealt with as discussed in the chapter on exposure. The exposure index of Kodachrome II can be varied, to produce normal—or in special cases—unusual experimental color effects. If you care to be conventional and confine your shooting to 9 A.M. until 3 P.M., you won't have to adjust film speed, since you will essentially always be dealing with the same type of contrasty lighting. But if you want to produce unusual pictures in color, shoot several experimental rolls in different lighting situations or of different subjects, and then decide on your own preferred E.I. for a given situation. This will probably be close to the manufacurer's rating of 25 for Kodachrome II Daylight Type, if you are shooting in very contrasty light, and may vary as high as 40 if illumination is very flat, as on an overcast day, and the subject is light in tone.

There are two very special kinds of lighting situations which require special mention, since the results when shooting in them are not what the inexperienced might expect. First, the mountains.

Meter readings at very high altitudes indicate exceptional brightness. With an incident meter, a recommended exposure may be as high as $f/16$ at 1/250 second with Kodachrome II Daylight Type rated at E.I. 25; this is true too for a reflected light reading taken from sunlit flesh tones. Don't go by it. If you expose as indicated, your transparencies will be slightly underexposed. The shadows will not be completely black as was the case with Kodachrome, but since mountain lighting is contrasty lighting with little atmospheric haze to bounce illumination back and forth and to illuminate the shadows you will still probably prefer slides exposed about ½ stop more than indicated by your meter.

The second situation is the beach on very bright days. Here, light sand reflects light back into the shadows, and there is usually a fine haze present which also cuts down contrast. You will probably find that the best transparencies you make are exposed about one stop less than indicated by an incident meter reading, or about as indicated by a reflected light reading. Keep in mind one other point for beach-scapes: Conventional over-all meter reading technique for landscapes is to point the meter slanting down at the ground to cut out the high illumination from the sky, and get a much truer indication of exactly how bright your scene will be.

For convenience, let's examine this, using two scenics as examples, page 44 and page 45. The picture on page 45 was made on a very bright day in the hills in Puerto Rico. The sky was metered at 400, the landscape at 200, and a close-up reading from my palm was 800. I followed the meter exactly. The correct exposure for Kodachrome II was $f/11$ and 1/60. In the beach scene, page 44, the sky again measured 400, my hand 800; but the sand, and water being extremely light, measured slightly above the 800 mark on the Weston dial. Here, correct exposure for Kodachrome II was $f/11$ and 1/125, despite the fact that the sky and hand readings were identical with those in the other situation: first, because the most important parts of the subject were very light, and second, because illumination in the shadows was great, and over-all reflectance was high.

For transparencies of equal density, take the tone of your subject matter into

44

account. Both photographs with Leica M3, 35mm f/2 Summicron.

FILTERS—A BRIEF CONSIDERATION

We will cover filters to be used with Kodachrome II film in detail in another chapter, but I would like to briefly discuss several musts for general outdoor work. Actually, no color film "sees" precisely as the eye sees. Recall that we discussed light as the form of radiant energy to which our eye is sensitive. But radiant energy exists in wave lengths longer and shorter than those which we can perceive. The longer wave lengths we feel as heat, but that is of little importance in color work since the Kodachrome II emulsion is not affected, at least not in any very important way, by energy in that part of the spectrum. The shorter wave lengths, or ultraviolet, however, do affect Kodachrome II as they do all photographic emulsions. Have you ever had the experience of taking a photograph on a slightly hazy day, but one on which you could see a distant object—a mountain, the Statue of Liberty from New York's Battery—perfectly clearly? If so, you were probably disappointed in the results. What appeared clear to your eye did not to the film, and chances are your mountain or the Statue of Liberty were well-nigh obscured. This was because of invisible ultra-violet light in the atmosphere. A number of manufacturers market filters designed to prevent ultraviolet light from reaching your film: Kodak's is called the Skylight Filter. A number of photographers leave this filter on the camera all the time. The Skylight Filter cuts out ultraviolet, extraneous blue light, and a minute portion of green, and if these wave lengths are not present, the filter has no effect at all, or perhaps only a slight warming effect. A Skylight or UV filter is highly recommended at high altitudes, on overcast or hazy days, and in open shade; in other lighting situations, as in these, it serves to protect your lens from dust, dirt, fingerprints, etc. Don't overlook the fact that it is easier to replace a scratched filter than to replace a damaged lens. The Skylight Filters have no filter factor; that is, no exposure compensation is needed if you use one. See page 69 for a simple test to determine whether or not you want to use one consistently.

Atmospheric haze and ultraviolet are especially troublesome when you are using long lenses. With normal, wide-angle, or near normal focal lengths, your subject will usually be fairly close to the camera, or at least most of it will be. But when you're using a telephoto lens, or shooting through binoculars or telescopes to bring distant objects up close, the trouble starts. During summer, when heat is reflected from the surface of the earth, distant objects will be distorted and possibly obscured by the refraction of light by air layers of different heat and density. This difficulty is all but insurmountable. Haze or UV filters, however, can be a big help in overcoming the effects of ultraviolet radiation, and you should under no circumstance attempt telephoto photography without one. Complete details on these filter, on ways of attaching them to your lens, and on any other filters which you may want to try with Kodachrome II appear in Chapter 7.

If you want to use just one type of film indoors and out you can convert Type A Kodachrome II for outdoors by using a Kodak Wratten Number 85 Conversion Filter. It is possible to use a filter with Kodachrome II Daylight Type for indoor use with floods; however, this filter, the Wratten Number 80B reduces film speed to about E.I. 10. The working film speed of Type A film with the Kodak Wratten 85 filter for shooting in daylight is the same as for Kodachrome II Daylight Type; hence, if you plan to shoot both indoors and out and don't want to change films, this combination is preferable.

Unless the front element of the lens on your camera is recessed in its mount, you should always use a lens hood when working indoors or out. The manufacturer of your camera either markets one himself, or can recommend one for the specific lens. Your local photographic dealer carries a variety, and hoods to fit every lens ever manufactured are put out by a number of independent manufacturers. Many of these hoods will screw into a filter adapter ring, replacing the outside of the ring itself. These are recommended. Light bouncing off the surface of a filter can do as much damage and create as much fog, as light hitting the front element of the lens. Kodachrome II can't tell the difference.

Practice hand holding the slow shutter speeds for available light shooting. Here, three tourists examine mosaics in church at Ravenna, Italy. Sole light source was window light. Kodachrome II Daylight Type exposure, 1/8 sec. at f/2, Leica M3, 50mm f/2 Summicron.

CHAPTER FIVE

Available Light

Kodachrome II Type A* opens up the available light situation to the photographer. Kodachrome Type A, with its E.I. of 16, was simply too slow for most available light situations. True, you could make a time exposure with your camera on a tripod; but if you were interested in scenes involving people, this meant that you had to confine your shooting to completely controlled situations, such as formal portaiture. And let's face it. If a formal portrait is what you're after, you'd be better off using floods than relying on the illumination which happens to be present.

Available light is the realm of the candid photographer. In color as in black-and-white, we are willing to overlook some technical imperfections if the people in the scene seem spontaneous, if they seem to have been photographed unawares.

If you have a camera with a lens of $f/2.8$ or faster, you will be able to cover a number of available light situations. The faster, of course, the better; the working 40 E.I. of Kodachrome II Type A, while amazing for a film of its quality, is still a far cry from the ratings of the black-and-white films now used for available light shooting. Most 35mm cameras, even the less expensive, have lenses of at least $f/2.8$; most 16mm movie cameras and 8mm cameras have at least $f/1.4$ as a maximum aperture, and lenses are available

* Since 35mm Kodachrome II Type A was not available at the time we went to press, all information on using it is based on extensive tests made with 16mm Kodachrome II Type A shot both as movies, and as stills in a 16mm GaMi ultraminiature camera. At press time, Eastman Kodak Co. had not announced when Kodachrome II Type A would be introduced.

with maximum apertures as wide as $f/0.9$. Most automatic cameras are not ideally suited for available light work. Their meters are not generally sufficiently sensitive for extremely low light; and special meter reading techniques, discussed later in the chapter should be used in many available light situations. Most of these cameras, however, can be used on bulb and you can choose your aperture, so they are suitable for available light work with time exposures, if you use an accessory meter. Or, if you are willing to limit your shutter speed to 1/30 second, you can use the flash setting with which you can vary aperture.

If you are interested in shooting candids at home, on the street, or working at all in low light situations, you will find one of the new supersensitive meters enormously helpful. The SEI meter, which has been marketed for a number of years, is excellent, but expensive. The Heiland Spot Meter is somewhat more sensitive than most other meters and it, like the Gossen Lunasix, is powered by a cadmium sulfide cell which, while increasing its sensitivity reduces its bulk. Another supersensitive meter is the Elwood, which is power-boosted by a tiny battery. For specifics on these meters, see the meter listing in Chapter 3.

I have been working with the Gossen Lunasix as an all-around meter. While it is somewhat bulkier than most meters, it is less so than the other super-sensitive meters on the market, and it is conveniently shaped to fit in a gadget bag or purse. And certainly it more than makes up in versatility for any inconvenience suffered because of its size.

Since the Lunasix is designed to be used as both an incident and reflected type meter without any accessories at all, it takes a split second to shift from one type of reading to another. It is accurate in any light situation, and since it can handle almost anything short of complete blackness in available light, there is no reason why it shouldn't be used consistently. If you are working out of doors and decide to go inside—to a museum, to a friend's home; anywhere, in short, where the light level is low—you are able to measure the light in both situations without having to carry boosters, change cells, pull slides, or do anything at all.

To be perfectly honest, probably the main reason (apart from its great sensitivity) that I prefer the Lunasix to other meters is that I have a propensity to misplace accesory items—lens caps, shades, filters, boosters, etc.—which are not attached to the camera or to the meter. Since the Lunasix comes in one piece and will stay that way unless you break it, I find it an ideal meter.

I do not mean to imply that all other meters have easily misplaced accessories which must be used for low light, that other meters are not sensitive, that other meters are not fairly compact and easy to carry. The Weston, the Norwood, the GE are all smaller; you don't need any accessories with the Weston, unless you want to use it as an incident light meter; the SEI and the Elwood are also very sensitive and have the added advantage of allowing you to make spot readings from small parts of your subject from a distance.

Let us discuss three general types of available light shooting: in people's homes; on the street at night; in theatres, arenas, stadiums.

AVAILABLE LIGHT IN YOUR HOME

I do not consider changing the position of an existing room light, or replacing a dim 40-watt bulb with a higher powered 150-watt bulb incompatible with the term available light. Often it may be considerably simpler—and less disrupting—to move a standing lamp, or to tilt its shade, than to ask your subject to move. Too, many homes are simply so dark that you will find it necessary to replace existing bulbs with stronger ones, even with the faster speed rating of Kodachrome II.

In the last chapter I discussed color temperature, and the factors affecting the color of daylight. The color temperature of various artificial light sources varies too, and the different watt bulbs each have different temperatures. The color temperature of a 50-watt bulb is about 2670K; a 100-watt, 2740K; a 200-watt, 2810K. Furthermore, Kodachrome Type A is balanced to be used with 3400K floods, not with these household tungsten bulbs. All of these color temperatures are approximate, since as the lamps are used their color temperature drops. The color temperature of a single lamp also varies with the voltage input. While most buildings are wired to provide a constant 110-volt circuit, there are fluctuations depending on the load. Using a long extension cord will also cut the voltage actually reaching the lamp, as will too many appliances on one line.

If you are concerned with improving the accuracy of the color of your Kodachrome II available light transparencies, I suggest that you invest in several light balancing filters. I will discuss filters in general in chapter 7, but a word about this series, which is specifically made to compensate for differences between the color temperature of a tungsten light source and the color temperature for which the film is balanced. There are two sets of these filters: the yellowish, warming Kodak Wratten 81 series, to be used when the color temperature of the light source is higher than the color temperature for which the film is balanced; and the bluish, cold Kodak Wratten 82 series, meant for use when the color temperature of the light source is lower than the color temperature for which the film is balanced. There are four filters in each series, designated Kodak Wratten 81-82, 81A-82A, 81B-82B, 81C-82C. The Wratten 81 filter will make a scene 100K warmer; the Wratten 81A, 200K warmer; the Wratten 81B, 300K warmer; the Wratten 81C, 400K warmer. These filters do have filter factors, however, and whenever you use them be sure to take the necessary exposure increase into account. A chart outlining the various light balancing filters and their effect, singly and in combination, appears on page 71.

But how do you know precisely how much, how many degrees Kelvin, a scene should be warmed or cooled for the color effect you want? Differences of several hundreds of degrees usually are not objectionable—or even evident—to the most experienced, let alone inexperienced color photographer as he looks at a scene—but he will see the difference in his trial slide or movie footage. There are just two answers: buy a color temperature meter; rely on experimentation, if you will be working in the same location; or install a voltage control device.

The first of these possibilities involves some cash outlay, since color temperature meters range in price from approximately $30 for about the least expensive, to hundreds of dollars for the most expensive. And most of the color temperature meters available to the amateur measure only the blue and red light, ignoring green and ultraviolet. If you want a color temperature meter just for use with tungsten illumination (where the imbalance between film and source will involve blue or red light only), a color temperature meter should be extremely useful. It won't, however, solve all of your outdoor picture-taking color balance problems — unless, of course, you can afford to invest a great deal of money for a professional instrument. Remember, none of these meters is more than a tool which will give you recommendations that you may not want to follow exactly in specific situations, any more than you would the light readings you take with your regular light meter.

Unless you do a great deal of available light shooting, it would be more reasonable simply to perform some experiments on your own than to invest in a special meter. Kodachrome II Type A, we know, is balanced for 3400K illumination. And we have learned that the color temperature from tungsten bulbs varies from about 2600K for 15-watt bulbs to 2900K for 100-watt bulbs. Shoot a roll of Type A film, making several exposures without a filter, and several with an 82C, which should cool the scene 400K (don't forget to increase exposure). The difference will be obvious—and if you find the unfiltered transparencies too red and those shot with the 82C too blue, try one of the other filters in the 82 series, which may produce results more to your taste.

Keep in mind the fact that correction to produce "normal" color balance in available light work may not look normal at all. Most of us are accustomed to warm available light photographs, and if you correct completely, your pictures will appear too blue.

One caution for all available light shooting: the light sources must all be of approximately the same color temperature. That is, you shouldn't mix illumination from, say, bluish fluorescents, which have a high color temperature, close to that of daylight, and regular tungsten bulbs unless it is for a very specific experimental purpose.

Fluorescents present special problems in shooting. All fluorescents used for general illumination do not have the same color temperature. Furthermore, their exact color temperature cannot be measured, since these lights emit a discontinuous spectrum, unlike other sources of illumination. For Daylight type tubes, use Kodachrome II Daylight Type, and as a starting point a CC-30M (see Chapter 7) and a CC-10Y filter, plus 1 stop. For white light fluorescents, use Kodachrome II Type A with a CC-10Y and a CC-30M filter, plus $\frac{1}{2}$ stop. For warm white bulbs use Kodachrome II Type A plus a CC-30M filter and $\frac{1}{2}$ stop. For cool white bulbs, Kodachrome II Type A with a CC-40Y and a CC-30M, plus $1\frac{1}{2}$ stops exposure increase. These recommendations are meant to be taken as a starting point only. When you examine the processed slides, you can adjust filtration at your next shooting if the color balance does not suit you.

OUTDOORS AT NIGHT

It is quite possible to make pictures of excellent quality shooting on brilliantly illuminated streets at night, with a shutter speed of 1/30 or 1/15 sec. or so with Kodachrome II Type A. To take accurate readings out of doors, you will definitely need one of the super-sensitive meters, and I suggest that you check the list appearing on page 31 for a rundown on them. One of the characteristics of Kodachrome II which is most helpful for outdoor night shooting is its latitude, for night scenes are usually very contrasty, with bright spots composed of the actual light sources, and shadows which are practically impenetrable to the eye. The standard exposure technique for night work is not to expose for the highlights (the light sources themselves), but for the most important area in which you want detail. By daylight standards the shadows should be underexposed. If you give it full exposure, the scene will look like daylight: and you are, after all, trying to create a night effect. Here, the professional procedure of bracketing is particularly helpful. Once you have determined your standard exposure, by estimation or meter reading, shoot one and two stops over and one and two stops under. Then, when you see the results, you will be able to judge for yourself which is best. And in your future night time shooting, your exposure choices can be guided by this experience.

For available light work both indoors and out you should have a tripod. A vast number are available from photographic dealers and my only suggestion as to which you should choose is based on the fact that it should be sturdy. There is a popular notion that the smaller and lighter the camera, the smaller and lighter the tripod is needed to support it. This simply is not true. Heavier cameras provide a stabilizing force by pressing down on the tripod. Small, light cameras require just as sturdy a tripod.

THEATRE AND SPECTACLES

Stage lights, are often sufficiently bright for you to be able to make an exposure with Kodachrome II. Here, the main difficulty is that of making a reading from the audience. One of the spot reading meters will be extremely helpful, as it will be for any situation where you cannot come up close to your subject.

A word about the circumstances under which it is advisable to take pictures at a dramatic performance. Most serious theatre-goers cannot help but be annoyed if a member of the audience stands up to take pictures, or takes more than a few. Even the quietest of shutters in a still camera will distract the people sitting in your immediate vicinity; those not so quiet can be heard by the full audience. First, if your camera does not have an extremely quiet shutter, give up the idea of taking pictures. If you are going to photograph at a regular performance, either stand at the back of the theatre and use a longer than normal lens; or take just a very few shots from your seat.

This holds, of course, for regular performances only. If you are interested in theatre photography, contact an amateur or semi-professional group in your vicinity. They will probably be delighted to have you photograph rehearsals, and will be generally cooperative.

There is more than sufficient illumination to photograph at outdoor sports, such as night football or baseball games with Kodachrome II. Often, however, these activities are lit by arc lights which have a color temperature close to but slightly higher than that of daylight. For such shooting, you should use Kodachrome II Daylight Type, probably without filtration. But if your results seem too blue, try a Kodak Skylight or possibly a Wratten 81 or even a Wratten 81A filter. Where the light is not strong enough to permit action stopping shutter speeds, try panning your camera or waiting for the peak of action, as explained in Chapter 2.

55

Use electronic flash outdoors for closeups of wild life. Thielemann made this picture with a Contarex, 85mm f/3.5 Tessar, at an aperture of f/22.

CHAPTER SIX

Artificial Light

While in some situations you will prefer to work with existing light, you can achieve a much greater degree of control and often much better photographs by using artificial light. You needn't invest in a lot of expensive equipment; and you shouldn't regard this way of working as involving such situations as you encounter at your local portrait photographer's. You can use artificial light so unobtrusively that your subjects won't even be affected by it. First, let's run over the types of lights which are available, their uses, so you can decide which will be the best for you.

Artificial lighting for stills can be divided into two main categories: flood and flash, which, of course, can be used only for stills. Two main types of lights are available for flood work. Photoflood lamps, which you put in a separate reflector, and reflector floods, which have their own reflector built in. These are the light sources for which your Kodachrome II Type A film is balanced at 3400K. Both types of photofloods are basically similar to the incandescent tungsten lamps you use for regular illumination; the difference is that they burn at a much higher voltage. This makes the filament hotter, raising the color temperature and the intensity of the light, and cutting the life of the bulb from the usual hundreds of hours to from four to six hours. The 3400K color temperature, however, is an average, and if you regard it as a constant, you may be disappointed in the results. The color temperature of photoflood lamps, like the household bulbs discussed in the last chapter, falls as the bulbs are used. For this reason, they aren't suitable for critical work. But they do offer an advantage in price, and the reflector floods are extremely portable and compact. Reflector spots are also available, similar to the floods, but with a more concentrated beam.

Some lights which look like photofloods are specifically meant for consistent photographic work. The color temperature of the light from these 3200K lamps is more nearly constant throughout their life, and they can be used with the proper filter (for completely accurate color) and Kodachrome II Type A film. The closest light-balancing filter for this purpose (see chart page 71) is the Kodak Wratten 82A, which will balance a source of 3180K for a film balanced at 3400K. Such differences (3180 to 3200K, or 20K) will not be apparent on the processed film, for there is a difference of about 50K towards the warm or cool side of normal, or a total latitude of 100K which won't be obvious to the most practiced and sensitive eye.

The 3200K lamps also have a considerably longer life than photofloods; about 35 to even 60 hours as opposed to the four to six expectancy mentioned above. Their only disadvantages are price (they are more expensive initially than floods, but this cost is offset by their longer life). Which reflector you choose to use with either floods or 3200K lamps will depend on the lighting effect you are after. A deep reflector with a narrow diameter will concentrate the beam; a wide reflector will spread it. For most indoor work, I suggest a large, wide reflector. The light will be more even, and cover a larger area, and will be better for most situations whether you plan to use the light direct or for bounce. A deep narrow reflector, however, will be helpful for dramatic effects, for instance, if you want to use extremely contrasty lighting for a man's portrait.

Flash illumination also falls into two main categories: regular flash bulbs, and electronic flash units. Expendable flash bulbs are available in a number of different sizes, and offer several advantages over electronic flash for the photographer who works only occasionally indoors. The first advantage is cost. The least expensive flash bulb costs about 8 cents; the least expensive electronic flash units cost about $23. Second, the light output of flash bulbs is considerably greater. The amount of light from one 25 cent flash bulb is equal to that from hundreds of dollars of electronic flash equipment.

Most flash bulbs contain aluminum, aluminum magnesium, or zirconium wire, oxygen under pressure, and a tiny filament connected to the terminals. When you fire the bulb, the filament is heated, the wire ignites and burns in a fraction of a second (reaching a very high temperature) and light is emitted. There are two types of these bulbs which will concern us here. The first: bulbs meant for use with all between-the-lens shutter cameras and focal plane shutter cameras at speeds of about 1/30 sec. or less. These include the AG baseless, with a light output of approximately 7000 lumens; the M-2, with a light output of approximately 7500 lumens; the M-5 and M-25 pinless, with a light output of approximately 16,000 lumens; the SM and SF gas-filled, with a light output of approximately 5000 lumens; the 5 and 25 bayonet base with a light output of approximately 20,000 lumens; the 11 and 40 screw base with a light output of approximately 33,000 lumens; the 22 and 2 screw base, with a light output of approximately 70,000 lumens; and the 50 or 3 screw base, with a light output of approximately 100,000 lumens.

The second: FP bulbs, for use with focal-plane shutter cameras at all speeds. These include the 6 and 26 bayonet base, with a light output of approximately 17,500 lumens and the 31 and 2-A screw base with a light output of approximately 81,000 lumens. The differences between regular and FP bulbs are explained by the fact that the rate of combustion depends on the thickness of the wire with which the lamp is filled. Bulbs for between-the-lens type shutters (with the exception of SM and SF) are filled with very fine wire, which reaches a high intensity in a very short time and is exhausted; FP lamps are filled with two sizes of wire, the thicker of which is consumed more slowly and at a relatively constant intensity. Note that the light from these bulbs lasts longer, but at no point is so bright as that from the bulbs for between-the-lens type cameras.

The type of bulb you will need depends on the camera you are using, or rather its shutter. The peak intensity of the bulb for between-the-lens type cameras is timed to coincide with the moment when the leaf shutter is fully open. The longer peak intensity necessary for focal plane shutters at speeds higher than 1/25 sec. is because at these speeds the shutters are never fully open. The size of the slit varies, and the illumination must be practically even as it makes the full trip across the film plane.

Both class M or S and FP flash bulbs have a color temperature of about 3800K. Since this is 400K higher than the light for which your Kodachrome II Type A is balanced, you may prefer to use a light-balancing filter over the lens. I want to reemphasize that the specific filter you choose will depend to a great degree on your own personal taste. While an 81C would theoretically be the correct filter, you may prefer the 81D, if you, like many other photographers, prefer warm flesh tones.

There are also amber-colored flash bulbs available which are meant for use specifically with Type A film, and blue bulbs for use with Daylight Type. However, these, since their color is from being dipped in a dye, do not always have precisely the same color temperature, and I don't see any reason for adding another variable factor to the ever-present differences in color balance coming from different emulsion batches and from processing. They are also more expensive than clear white flash bulbs. You can ensure more consistent results by using the clear bulbs and one of the light balancing filters. Blue flash bulbs will, of course, come in handy if you do very little flash work, and want to take just an occasional flash picture using Kodachrome II Daylight Type. They should also be used if you want to use flash as a fill when photographing outdoors against the light.

The second major type of flash illumination is electronic flash. If you plan to do a considerable amount of flash work, I highly recommend buying an electronic flash unit.

The general quality of the light from electronic flash units makes them ideal for both black-and-white and color work. The light is relatively soft compared to the illumination from regular flash bulbs. Since its color temperature is close to that of daylight, you can use it with Kodachrome II Daylight Type, with or without a slight warming filter. The color temperature and the intensity of illumination is constant with a single unit, so once you have determined the best filter for you, you don't have to worry about the possibility of inconsistent results.

Another advantage of electronic flash is its extremely short duration. A single flash lasts from about 1/500 to 1/2000 sec. on most amateur units, the specific duration depending on the unit you buy. With electronic flash, there is far less danger of unsharpness from camera movement, or subject movement with any but the most active subjects. They can be used at all shutter speeds with leaf shutters using the "X" setting. With focal plane shutters the maximum usable shutter speed is 1/25 to 1/60 sec., depending on the camera. The new all metal shutters in the Konica F and FS cameras permit use of electronic flash at 1/125 sec.

Guide numbers supplied by the manufacturer very often will not be completely accurate. Some manufacturers publish a considerably higher guide number than you will find practical to use. With black and white, the error will not usually be noticeable. When you buy a unit, I suggest that you bracket exposures on your first roll of film, shooting one and two stops wider open than the aperture indicated by using the manufacturer's guide number. It is most unlikely that you will find your transparencies overexposed if you follow the manufacturer's recommendation: hence, forget about bracketing in the other direction for the time being. Units are usually tested, I suspect, under optimum conditions, calculated to make it possible to assign the highest possible guide number to the unit (i.e., small room, white walls, ceiling, etc.). The workable guide number, of course, will depend on the circumstances under which you are working, and we shall cover this in greater detail later in this chapter. Most electronic flash units can be used on regular AC household current. Using the units on AC, however, is obviously practical only when working with relatively static subjects, since the cord to the wall outlet can be a hazard if many people are walking around.

MOVIES—A SPECIAL LIGHTING PROBLEM

Movies present a special problem when working indoors. The artificial light source must be floods or 3200K lamps. These usually are mounted on bar light units, a number of which are available, which take two or four lights. Recommended guide numbers appear on the back of these units (also see chart page 62). Filter recom-

PHOTOFLOOD TABLE, 2-LAMP BAR*

With 3-lamp bar, use lens opening ½ stop smaller. With a
4-lamp bar, use lens opening a whole stop smaller.

LENS OPENINGS	200-WATT (DAN) LAMPS		300- OR 375-WATT (BEP OR BFA) LAMPS	
	KODACHROME FILM, TYPE A	KODACHROME II FILM, TYPE A	KODACHROME FILM, TYPE A	KODACHROME II FILM, TYPE A
f/8	—	—	—	3½'— 5'
f/5.6	—	4' — 6'	—	5' — 7'
f/4	3'— 5'	6' — 8½'	4' — 6'	7' —10'
f/2.8	5'— 7'	8½'—12'	6' — 8½'	10' —14'
f/2.3	6'— 8½'	10' —14'	7' —10'	12' —17'
f/1.9	7'—10'	12' —17'	8½'—12'	15' —21'

*For new lamps, beams superimposed. After burning lamps for 1 hour, use lens
opening ½ stop larger. After 2 hours, use next larger opening.
Reproduced with permission from the copyrighted Kodak booklet, "How to Make
Good Home Movies," p. 50.

mendations, of course, are the same as with stills. The camera is
attached to the bar itself, and the lamp moved with the camera as
the photographer changes angle or camera-to-subject distance. Most
of the units have a provision for changing the direction of the
illumination so that the light can be directed at wall or ceiling for
bounce.

One of the problems with indoor movie making is that of
getting consistently correct exposure so that you have equal exposures for each scene you make. While, as we have discussed,
Kodachrome II's extraordinary exposure latitude does compensate
for exposure errors, this doesn't mean that an error hasn't been
made and that differences in exposure are not noticeable. Since
you view your 35mm slides as single, not continuous, images,
variations in exposure are really not so important. But with movies
you will want to splice footage together, and you may want to use
different angles for different scenes which you make during one
shooting. You want these all to blend without noticeable differences,
either in color or in lighting contrast. I seriously suggest that if you

plan to do much indoor movie making you investigate the possibility of getting a device which will insure constant voltage. If you can use bulbs which are consistently under the actual voltage of your line (this must be checked with a voltmeter), you can use a simple rheostat to keep voltage constant. There are also special transformers available which insure constant current, and with which you can step up line voltages. These, however, are much more expensive. If you are serious, however, about indoor movie making, it may be well worth the price.

Another interesting and highly useful unit for both stills and movies is the colortran, which makes an ordinary light bulb burn at extremely high intensity. Two 150-watt bulbs, for instance, can supply 3500 watts of illumination. If you need a great deal of light but do not have heavy duty wiring, this device will solve the problem. Prices for colortrans vary from about $160 to $300. With the ColorTrue Converter Model CT, you can choose either 3200K or 3400K, and use a total of 900 watts. Such elaborate—and expensive—devices are hardly necessary for any amateur whose indoor picture taking consists of taking shots of his family.

The Sylvania Sun Gun (Westinghouse and General Electric make similar units) is an excellent unit for indoor movie making. It is made to be used in the same fashion as a regular bar light; that is, it attaches to the camera. It may be mounted on a light stand, however, and its head swivels easily for direct or bounce light. Its light output is equal to that of a multiple bar light, and its color temperature is 3400K, that for which your film is balanced. Its life is over twice that of photoflood lamps.

Now that we have covered some of the specific types of lights available for you to use indoors, we'll discuss the basic ways to use them with Kodachrome II for better stills and movies.

One of the most important characteristics of Kodachrome II both Daylight Type and Type A is its good latitude for indoor work. In order to understand this, let's consider for a moment the way light works. The intensity of light from a single source varies in inverse proportion to the square of the distance from source to object. To put it simply, let's consider a theoretical situation. Suppose you are making a portrait using one flood placed four feet from your subject. If you take a close-up reading of the face, the recommended exposure is $f/8$ and $1/100$; the reading on the Weston dial is 100. Now, move the lamp to a distance of eight feet, and take a close-up reading again. You expected a reading of 50, since you have doubled the distance. But the reading you get is 25, the correct exposure $f/8$ and $1/25$, or $1/100$ at $f/4$. Although the distance is twice as great, the exposure required is four times as great.

It is obvious, then, that if you are making pictures indoors and are using direct light, the intensity of light throughout the room will be extremely uneven. If you're photographing a group at a party, and one person is four feet from the camera, another at six feet, a third and fourth at 10 feet, how do you calculate exposure? Suppose you are using electronic flash, the most convenient and likely illumination for such a situation. Suppose the guide number for your electronic flash gun is 80 with Kodachrome II Daylight Type. The three correct $f/$numbers for the three different light-to-subject distances would be between $f/16$ and $f/22$ (four feet); between $f/11$ and $f/16$ (six feet); and $f/8$ (ten feet). This is an extremely wide range—almost three stops—and it indicates the light which will reach your nearest subject will be 16X that which reaches the people 10 feet from you. With Kodachrome film this would have been impossible; with Kodachrome II, it is still undesirable, but you will be able to make a compromise — say, shoot at $f/12.6$—and get a recognizable picture.

A better solution for most indoor picture taking situations where your subject is on more than one plane in depth is to use bounce light. The film speed of Kodachrome II is high enough to allow it to be used in average sized rooms, provided you shoot using a fairly wide aperture. Any light source can be bounced off ceiling or walls. As mentioned before, the light output of even the smallest flash bulb is greater than that with electronic flash units. Therefore, since light is cut down enormously when you bounce it, you may find the use of flash bulbs better than electronic flash.

For bounce flash work you will have to calculate your own guide number. Here's how to do it. Keep in mind that a number of different factors will affect the results—color and tone of a reflecting surface, in particular—and that some experimentation

Without and (below) with a Kodak Pola-Screen and four times as much exposure. Note the dramatic effect of the darkened blue sky and the increased color saturation in the leaves. From transparencies taken at Yosemite National Park by Ansel Adams.

Kodachrome II, normal exposure: In supersaturated colors, lower left, yellow, blue, red are clean, true. Note slight yellow coloration in lower right panel's top left.

Kodachrome II, underexposure: Compared to normal above, overexposure below, colors differ only slightly from Kodachrome. Yellows still have better differentation.

Kodachrome II, overexposure: Supersaturated color, lower left, is only slightly lighter than normal. Yellows, reds still retain good differentation. Overexposure is obviously well tolerated.

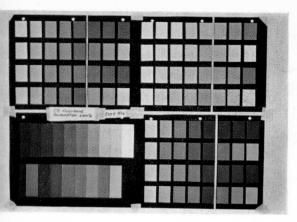

Kodachrome, normal exposure: Supersaturated yellow and red are orangy, blue muddy, light yellows colorless. Compare muddy green, bottom right, with K II. Grays show less gradations.

Kodachrome, underexposure: Colors appear slightly darker than in K II. Underexposure may render blue deeper: underexposed water may go darker with K than K II.

Kodachrome, overexposure: Everything is pale, showing that K has less latitude than K II. Note almost complete absence of yellow, indicating badly washed-out skin tones.

COLOR RENDITION: SOME DIFFERENCES ARE SLIGHT, OTHERS ARE MAJOR

Kodachrome II: Exposure reading from neutral gray card advised f/8, 1/100 sec. with Kodachrome II's exposure index (E.I.) of 25. Film's latitude kept shadows open and rendered detailed highlights well. Look at sand in shadows of children, right, facial tone on shadow sides of all children's faces. Also see brilliance of yellow dress, correct rendition of blue water, green in girl's dress, right.

Kodachrome: Calculating exposure in exactly same manner but using E. I. of 10, vastly different result was obtained under exactly same lighting conditions as above. Exposure was 1/100, f/4.5. Shadows are deep and filled in, entire picture is quite contrasty. Since film has less latitude, water is underexposed and therefore deeper than normal. Look what's happened to the yellow and green dresses.

CONTRAST: IN SOME DRAMATIC INSTANCES NEW FILM LACKS REAL PUNCH

Kodachrome II: Unlimbering her matched twin Leica M3 cameras quickly in Puerto Rico, Patricia Caulfield caught this rainbow against dramatic sky at f/9.5, 1/100 sec, using a reading from neutral gray card. While small aperture rendered excellent depth sharpness (note small shrub in foreground) and greens are differentiated from yellows, contrast in the sky itself is flatter.

Kodachrome: With exposure of f/4.5, 1/100 sec. a shot was made which matched overall gradation of picture above. Notice how shallow depth of field cuts down foreground detail, green is muddy and contrasts poorly with yellow. But look! the sky is definitely more dramatic because of inherently greater contrast in older Kodachrome. Not one shot in the whole K II exposure series equaled this sky.

SHARPNESS: NEW FILM'S BETTER BUT
YOU NEED A MICROSCOPE TO SEE IT

Kodachrome II: Here's part of a 35mm shot magnifed approx. 20X (the equivalent of a 20 x 30-in. print from full neg.). Unsharpness is due to the tremendous enlargement.

Kodachrome: Aside from warmer background, can you see any difference from shot above? Movies are different.

will be necessary. First, measure the distance between flash gun and ceiling, wall, or other reflecting surface from which you will bounce the light. Then, measure the distance from reflector to the subject. Add these two distances. Divide this total into the guide number for your flash bulb or electronic flash unit. Use an f/number two stops larger for your actual exposure, since some of the illumination will not reach your subject. If you are photographing in a large room, you may have to open the aperture as much as three or four stops more than indicated.

Bounce light works with color films only if the ceiling and walls are white. As discussed before in chapter 3, when the light illuminating a subject is reflected from a colored surface, the subject appears tinted in that shade. If your ceiling is a pale green or blue, your subjects will be pale green or blue in the transparency if you bounce the light from the ceiling.

ELECTRIC-EYE CAMERAS

Electric-eye cameras can be used successfully for indoor color work. I do suggest, however, that you do some experimentation with bounce light if you are using one of these cameras, and plan to use it on automatic. The reason for this is easily understood if you consider our discussion of light falloff from a point source (pages 63 and 64). (This holds true only, of course, if you are working with floods. Obviously, if you are using flash or electronic flash for still photographs, the camera must be set for flash work, in which case you must set the aperture, just as you would with the non-automatic cameras.) The meter on your electric-eye camera will take an over-all reading of the scene, and if your subjects are in front of a dark background or in the center of a fairly large room, the electric eye mechanism will not compensate for the large area which is relatively unilluminated. Your transparencies or footage will be overexposed. With still cameras you can compensate for this easily by using the close-up reading technique suggested for back light. With movies, the best solution is bouncing the light.

You will need a fast lens to photograph outdoors at night. This plaza in San Sebastian, Puerto Rico, could be filmed at f/1.4 on Kodachrome II Type A.

CHAPTER SEVEN

Filters

White light is actually composed of three primary colors: red, green, and blue. We—and our films—"see" an object as red because this object absorbs the green and blue wave lengths and reflects the red. A filter works in a similar fashion. A red filter looks red because it transmits (as opposed to reflecting) only red light, and absorbs green and blue.

In other words, filters do not *add* their color to a scene. They *subtract* colors other than their own. Specifically:

A red *filter*	*transmits* red	*absorbs* blue *and* green
blue	blue	red green
green	green	red blue
yellow (red, green)	red, green	blue
magenta (red, blue)	red, blue	green
cyan (blue, green)	blue, green	red

In actuality, most of the colors we see in nature are not pure. We may observe an object as red, or blue: but it almost always contains some elements of other colors as well. This is also true of filters. While dyes used are as close to the pure color as the filter manufacturers can make them, they do transmit small portions of the wave lengths which they theoretically should absorb. But this is of small practical importance.

Since filters remove some of the light reflected from your subject before it strikes the film, it is necesary to make some compensation in exposure from that indicated by a meter reading from the subject. All filters except haze, UV and skylight filters (see below) have a number called a filter factor, which indicates the number of times the exposure must be increased when the filter is in use. Actually, these filter factors are approximate, and must be adjusted to suit the type of lighting. If you are exposing a film to a light source which is predominantly red, for example, and have a cyan filter over the lens, all—or practically all—of the light which can be reflected from your subject will be absorbed by the filter.

F/stop Compensation for Filter Factors

Filter Factor	1.2	1.5	1.7	2	2.5	3	4	5	6	8	12	16	25
Open by (f/stop)	$\frac{1}{3}$	$\frac{2}{3}$	$\frac{2}{3}$	1	$1\frac{1}{3}$	$1\frac{2}{3}$	2	$2\frac{1}{3}$	$2\frac{2}{3}$	3	$3\frac{1}{3}$	4	$4\frac{1}{3}$

From "Filter Guide" by Norman Rothschild and Cora Wright, published by Amphoto.

For the most part, you will be using filters with Kodachrome II either to balance the illumination to match the color balance of the film for "normal" appearing transparencies; or to create a difference, or exaggerate an existing difference between color balance of light source and of the film for purposes of experimentation or interpretation. There are, also, several kinds of filters which you will find useful which are for entirely different purposes and do not affect color balance. Before discussing construction of filters, filter manufacturers, and how to attach filters to your camera, let's examine the filters or groups of filters about which you should know in order to get the best results from your Kodachrome II under any and all conditions.

1) Skylight, UV, Haze. These filters are all designed for outdoor use to remove excess blue from the scene, and to cut out ultraviolet. Probably the best for use with Kodachrome II Daylight Type is the Skylight (which is a pale pink or magenta in color and will have a slight warming effect on your transparencies. Since the color balance of Kodachrome II compensates for the excess blue common on many overcast days or in shadows—conditions for

The Warmth and Coolness of Common Light Sources

LIGHT SOURCE		Color Temperature Degrees Kelvin
Warmest	Candle or Kerosene Lamp Flame	1900°
	Carbon-Filament Lamp	2100°
	Vacuum Tungsten Lamp or Acetylene Flame	2360°
	Household Tungsten Lamp—40-60 Watt	2760-2790°
	—100 Watt	2860°
	3200K Studio Floods	3200°
	Photoflood Lamps	3400°
	"Warm White" Fluorescent Lamp	3500°
	Electric Arc, Solid Carbons	3750°
	Clear Flash Lamps	3800°
	"Cool White" Fluorescent Lamp	4500°
	Sunlight, before 9 AM, after 3 PM	5000°
	Sunlight, 9 AM to 3 PM (Average)	5500°
	Blue Flash Lamps	6000°
	Electronic Flash	5500-7000°
	Heavily Overcast Sky	6500°
	Lightly Overcast Sky	7500°
	Blue Sky { Hazy	9000°
Coldest	In Shadow	12000°
	Clear	25000°

From "Filter Guide" by Norman Rothschild and Cora Wright, published by Amphoto.

which this filter is expressly recommended—the Skylight filter is not as important as it was with the original Kodachrome film. I would suggest shooting several different scenes with and without the filter (unless you are just beginning to shoot color, you probably already have a Skylight filter) and compare the results to determine if you want to use it. Many color photographers leave this filter on the lens at all times, not just when conditions require its use. It has little effect in general, and it serves to protect the lens from dust, fingerprints, scratches, etc. One other point should be made in connection with this filter: you have heard, probably, about certain lenses being "warm" or "cool" but chances are you have never stopped to analyze the lenses you use in terms of color

69

APPROXIMATELY EQUIVALENT FILTERS FOR COLOR

	Kodak Accura Enteco Gallinger Tiffen Walz	Ednalite	Harrison & Harrison	Approximate Exposure Increase in f/stops*	
SALMON COLORED	85B	Chrom B	C-5	2	
	85	Chrom A	C-4	1½	WARMING
	85C	Chrom F	C-2	1	
PALE YELLOWISH	81EF	CTY-6	C-1	⅔	
	81D	CTY-5	C-¾	⅔	
	81C	CTY-4	C-½	⅓	
	81B	CTY-3	C-¼	⅓	
	81A	CTY-2	C-⅛	⅓	
	81	CTY-1	C-⅛	⅓	
PALE BLUISH	82	CTB-1	B-⅛	⅓	
	82A	CTB-2	B-¼	⅓	COOLING
	82B	CTB-3	B-½	⅔	
	82C	CTB-4	B-½	⅔	
BLUE	80C	80C	B-2	1	
	80B	80B	B-4	2	

*These figures are to be used as a rough guide only. The exact factor will depend on which filter, film and light-source combination is used. Always check manufacturers' data carefully, then make your own practical tests.

Filter equivalency in this chart is based on filter use. Due to differences in manufacture, systems of calculation and dyes used, it is impossible to specify exact filter equivalents.

From "Filter Guide" by Norman Rothschild and Cora Wright, published by Amphoto.

KODAK LIGHT BALANCING FILTERS

Color	Wratten Number	Exposure Increase in Stops*	Color Temperature of Source		Mired Interval
			Converted to 3200 K	Converted to 3400 K	
Bluish	82C + 82C	1⅓	2490 K	2610 K	—89
	82C + 82B	1⅓	2570 K	2700 K	—77
	82C + 82A	1	2650 K	2780 K	—65
	82C + 82	1	2720 K	2870 K	—55
	82C	⅔	2800 K	2950 K	—45
	82B	⅔	2900 K	3060 K	—32
	82A	⅓	3000 K	3180 K	—21
	82	⅓	3100 K	3290 K	—10
No Filter Necessary			3200 K	3400 K	—
Yellowish	81	⅓	3300 K	3510 K	9
	81A	⅓	3400 K	3630 K	18
	81B	⅓	3500 K	3740 K	27
	81C	⅓	3600 K	3850 K	35
	81D	⅔	3700 K	3970 K	42
	81EF	⅔	3850 K	4140 K	52

*These values are approximate. For critical work, they should be checked by practical test, especially if more than one filter is used.

Reproduced with permission from the copyrighted Kodak booklet, "Kodak Filters and Pola Screens," p. 19.

balance results. You won't notice the differences in color balance between transparencies made with the warmest and coolest lenses on the market — unless you are looking for it. But differences are there, and probably if your lens is of the "warm" variety, you will find the consistent use of the Skylight filter undersirable; if "cool," you may want to use it all of the time. My final bit of advice regarding the Skylight filter is not to use it unless there is a specific reason for doing so based on prior practical tests.

2) *Conversion filters.* Several of these filters are actually part of the light-balancing series discussed below, but are discussed separately here in relation to their specific application in enabling you to use Kodachrome II with completely different lights than that for which it is balanced.

Backgrounds can be a problem when photographing pets—or people. Lighting contrast provides a solution: natural backlight from window burns out background detail. (Kodachrome II exposure, f/2 and 1/15.) Photograph by Patricia Caulfield with Topcon C, 100mm Auto Topcon lens.

To use:

Kodachrome II Daylight Type with 3400K photofloods: Kodak Photoflood Filter (80B)

Kodachrome II Daylight Type with clear flash bulbs: Kodak Photoflash Filter (80C).

Kodachrome II Daylight Type with 3200K lamps: Kodak Photoflood Filter (80B) and Kodak Light Balancing Filter (82A).

Kodachrome II Type A with clear flash bulbs: Kodak Light Balancing Filters (81C, 81D)

Kodachrome Film Type A with Daylight: Kodak Daylight Filter for Kodak Type A color films (85)

3) *Light Balancing Series.* These filters are usually used to compensate for differences in color temperature between the illumination and the light for which the film is balanced. While they are primarily meant for use with tungsten light and Type A films, they also may be used out of doors with Kodachrome II Daylight Type. See chart page 71 for a complete list of filters which are available, and their conversion effect on a light source. As you can see, the Kodak Wratten 82 series, which is blue, raises the effective color temperature of the light source while the yellowish Wratten 81 series lowers it. Eastman Kodak Co. very aptly points out in its databook "Kodak Filters and Pola Screens" that the term color temperature must be used with extreme caution particularly in this context since it gives information on the color of the source only, and not on its spectral energy distribution, which is of extreme importance in terms of its photographic effect. A specific film is balanced not only

LIGHT ► FILM ▼		Sunlight plus Skylight—Average	Open Shade, Marine, Cloudy, Distant Scenes Reddish	Late P.M. or Early A.M. Sunlight—	Electronic Flash	Blue Flashbulbs	Clear Wire Filled Flash (3800K)	Photofloods (3400K)	SM, SF Flash (3300K)	Studio Floods (3200K)	Amber Flash (Dura, Solar— 3200K)	Fluorescents			
												Daylight	White	Warm White	Cool White
KODACHROME II	Filter	None	1A	82A	None	None	80C	80B	N.R.	80B+82A	N.R.	20R	N.R.	N.R.	N.R.
	E.I.	25	25	20	25	80*	80*	12	N.R.	8	N.R.	16	N.R.	N.R.	N.R.
KODACHROME II TYPE A	Filter	85	85	85	N.R.	N.R.	81C	None	None	82A	None	N.R.	30M+10Y	30M	30M+40Y
	E.I.	25	25	25	N.R.	N.R.	150	40	90	32	150	N.R.	20	20	20

Above, a simple to use chart which will enable you to shoot your Kodachrome II in almost any type of light. The filters listed for use with fluorescent lighting are all of the Color Compensating type (see chart page 74), but the designation "CC" has been omitted to save space. Elsewhere, filters are numbered according to the Wratten system. The 1A filter is elsewhere in this book referred to as the Skylight filter. Numbers under clear flashbulbs used in the approximate reflector are approximate guide numbers for No. 5, 25, M5 and M25 lamps; under blue flashbulbs for No. 5B, 25B, M5B and M25B lamps, and under SM and SF for these lamps. Courtesy Modern Photography, compiled by Norman Rothschild.

KODAK COLOR COMPENSATING FILTERS

Peak Density	Yellow (Absorbs Blue)	Exposure Increase in Stops*	Magenta (Absorbs Green)	Exposure Increase in Stops*	Cyan (Absorbs Red)	Exposure Increase in Stops*
.05	CC05Y†	—	CC05M†	⅓	CC05C†	⅓
.10	CC10Y†	⅓	CC10M†	⅓	CC10C†	⅓
.20	CC20Y†	⅓	CC20M†	⅓	CC20C†	⅓
.30	CC30Y	⅓	CC30M	⅔	CC30C	⅔
.40	CC40Y†	⅓	CC40M†	⅔	CC40C†	⅔
.50	CC50Y	⅔	CC50M	⅔	CC50C	1

Peak Density	Red (Absorbs Blue and Green)	Exposure Increase in Stops*	Green (Absorbs Blue and Red)	Exposure Increase in Stops*	Blue (Absorbs Red and Green)	Exposure Increase in Stops*
.05	CC05R†	⅓	CC05G	⅓	CC05B	⅓
.10	CC10R†	⅓	CC10G	⅓	CC10B	⅓
.20	CC20R†	⅓	CC20G	⅓	CC20B	⅔
.30	CC30R	⅔	CC30G	⅔	CC30B	⅔
.40	CC40R†	⅔	CC40G	⅔	CC40B	1
.50	CC50R	1	CC50G	1	CC50B	1⅓

*These values are approximate. For critical work, they should be checked by practical test, especially if more than one filter is used.

Reproduced with permission from the copyrighted Kodak booklet "Kodak Filters and Pola Screens," p. 21.

for the color temperature of the source with which it is meant to be used, but also for the spectral energy distribution of that source. There is another method and set of filters, called the decamired system, which is also meant for light balancing. As you can see from the Kodak Light Balancing Filter Chart, the Wratten 81 and 82 series filters are also assigned a mired value. We will take up the decamired system in detail later in this chapter.

4) *Color Compensating Filters.* These filters (see chart above) can be used singly or in combination to produce almost any over-all color cast which you desire in a transparency. The density of each filter is indicated by the numbers in the filter name, and is measured at the wave length of maximum absorption. The density of a cyan filter, for example, indicates only the amount of red illumination which the dye absorbs, not the density of the gelatin in which the dye is dispersed nor the density of the glass in which the gelatin is mounted.

Color compensating filters, while intended to correct for abnormal lighting conditions and to produce normal appearing transparencies, offer great possibilities for creative experimentation. When used for this purpose, there are of course no rules—and there can be no specific filter recommendations. It's all up to you.

Color compensating filters—or the light-balancing filters mentioned above—can also be used when you are projecting your slides if you want to correct or change the color balance of your transparency. There are several ways of doing this. You can attach the filter in a filter holder over the projector's lens, just as you would attach it to the camera's lens if you were taking a picture. Tiffen and Enteco make the Trans pro and the Perfector respectively. These are filter attachments for slide or movie projectors to warm or cool the light. This method is best if you want to change the color balance of a number of transparencies, or of a length of movie footage. The other method, for individual transparencies, is to mount a piece of gelatin filter with the slide in glass. Methods of mounting will be covered in a later chapter.

There is a specific use for one of the color compensating filters which deserves special mention. The CC30R is marketed by one filter manufacturer as the Vistadome filter. This filter corrects for the greenish color of the windows found in many buses and special trains, and requires a different factor depending on whether you are shooting upwards through the densest part of the glass (about 2⅔ f/number increase) or through the less dense side windows (about 2 stops).

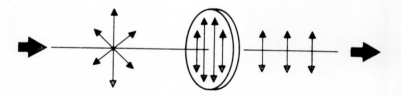

Polarizing filters only pass rays vibrating in same direction as "slats." Maximum effect is achieved when filter is rotated ninety degrees and most of polarized light is blocked.
From "The Nikon Manual" by George B. Wright, published by Universal Photo Books.

5) *Polarizing filters.* In appearance, polarizing filters resemble the grey neutral density filters discussed below. Their effect, however, is entirely different. Polarizing filters are used for two purposes: to darken sky (see illustration) and to remove or subdue reflections. In color work, they offer the only method for darkening skies without affecting the other colors in a scene except to remove reflections. When sky light reflections are removed from many objects —leaves, buildings, etc.,—they are revealed in their fully saturated colors. (NOTE: the sky should be clear. The effect of the filter is decreased by haze.) The polarizing filter does absorb ultraviolet. By doing this and removing reflected blue sky light from water droplets in the air, it can actually sometimes penetrate mild, distant haze. Any degree of darkness can be obtained, the variations determined by the angle of the screen. The effect of the screen can be easily observed by holding the filter to your eye and rotating it: the sky will appear darker or lighter as you turn the screen. The indicator handle on the filter—if yours has one—indicates maximum darkening effect when pointed at the sun. Most polarizing filters—those made by

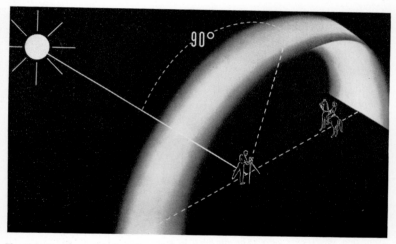

The Pola-Screen can darken the white band of sky. Maximum darkening of the sky takes place in a region at approximately right angles to a line extending from the sun to the camera. Reproduced with permission from the copyrighted Kodak booklet "Kodak Filters and Pola Screens," p. 35.

Eastman Kodak Co., Tiffen, Enteco, Walz, etc.—can be obtained with viewers which attach to the screen so that you can see the exact photographic effect. The filter works in a similar way with reflections from non-metallic objects. Look through the filter, turn it, and the reflection will disappear and return, if you are at the proper angle to the object.

How—and why—does this filter have this effect on skies and on reflections? Examine the illustration on page 75. Ordinary light rays vibrate in all directions; light rays which are polarized vibrate in one direction only. The polarizing filter transmits light which is vibrating in only one direction. Some of the light from certain portions of the sky (at right angles to the sun) and from reflections from non-metallic objects (at about 35 degrees from the subject) is polarized; therefore, it will be transmitted or absorbed by your polarizing filter, depending on how it is rotated. Obviously, the use of this filter dictates that you stand at a certain angle to your subject, since it is only when the subject is viewed at this angle that the light is polarized.

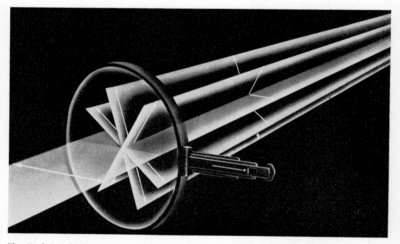

The Kodak Pola-Screen allows light vibrating in only one direction to pass through it. The resultant light ray is polarized and vibrates in one plane only—in line with the Pola-Screen handle. Reproduced with permission from the copyrighted Kodak booklet "Kodak Filters and Pola Screens," p. 35.

Like any other filter, the polarizing filter requires an increase in exposure, in other words, it has a filter factor. The increase in exposure depends on the degree of rotation of the filter, and also on the specific unit, varying according to the manufacturer's recommendations from 2½ to 4X.

CALCULATING EXPOSURE

The recommended filter factor with polarizing filters is calculated to give you the right exposure for foreground subject matter. You must exercise caution in taking your initial meter reading, however, and *not measure the reflection*, but the actual subject. Best method is to use an incident light meter, or to use the substitute method for reflected light readings.

One special—but very important—use of polarizing filters is for movie fades, the effect when a scene gradually darkens to black, or gradually appears from a dark screen. Here, two polarizing filters are mounted together. Filters with handles are easiest to use, since when handles are on top of or opposite one another, the maximum amount of light is transmitted; when handles are at 90 degrees to one another, the minimum amount of light is transmitted. The technique is simple: to have scenes fade out, simply start with the handles superimposed, gradually rotate one until it is at right angles to the other; to fade in, start with the handles at 90°, and move one until they are superimposed.

Incidentally, while the above recommendations are meant for outdoor use, polarizing filters are useful for indoor work too, since several lighting devices enable you to polarize illumination at will. Enteco and Tiffen made a polarizing filter (the Polarflash and Flash-Pol, respectively) which fits over a flash gun or electronic flash unit; Kodak makes the Pola-Light, basically a flood with a built-in polarizing filter. With any of these devices, you can have complete control over reflections when working by artificial light. This device also requires a polarizer on the camera lens.

6) *Neutral density filters.* Like the Polarizing filters, neutral density filters are meant for use with both black-and-white and color films. Their standard use is in situations which are too brightly illuminated—at the beach, or in a brilliantly lit snow scene—for

you to be able to photograph even with your lens stopped down to minimum aperture and with shutter set at the highest possible speed. Actually, although Kodachrome II is fast, it isn't so fast as to require the use of a neutral density filter, except under special circumstances or for special effects with most still cameras. A neutral density filter may be necessary for use with movie cameras, however, where the usual shutter speed for 16 frames is around 1/30. If the minimum aperture of your camera is $f/16$, your film may be overexposed when you shoot light colored subjects in very bright sun. And even if your camera does have $f/22$ as a minimum aperture, you will be limited to this, virtually eliminating any possibility of creative control through varying aperture. Any cinematographer interested in creative movie making would be well advised to invest in several neutral density filters, which would give him the still photographer's control over aperture, hence depth of field. For still photography, neutral density filters are particularly useful if you want to use fairly long exposures in bright sun, or want to use a wide aperture for limited depth of field. Neutral density filters come in a number of densities, and can be used in combination to produce almost any degree of absorption. The top chart on page 80 shows you the correct neutral density filter to use when light is too bright for the maximum aperture of your camera; the bottom chart on page 80 shows you the correct filter to use when you want to use a wider aperture than illumination permits.

7) *Black-and white filters.* Why mention black-and-white filters in a book on a color film? Simply because they can be used with color—for purely experimental purposes. Try shooting Kodachrome II through a green or a red or a blue filter: your results will be monochromatic, green or red or blue, hardly the effect you'll be after if you're taking pictures of your latest offspring to send to your relatives, but possibly highly effective if you're trying to cop first prize at your club's monthly competition, get an assignment for a creative color essay from a national magazine, or sell an agency on an idea for a campaign. Here, you should certainly experiment with exposure, using the manufacturer's recommended black and white filter factor as a starting point. Also try some double and triple exposures using a differently colored filter for each.

TIFFEN NEUTRAL DENSITY SELECTOR CHART I

In flash photograph at close range the light is often so bright that overexposure will result even when the smallest f/stop is used and the fastest shutter speed employed. In such instances a Tiffen Neutral Density Filter is used to reduce the amount of light reaching the film.

Another use for Tiffen Neutral Density Filters is in movie making with high speed color or black-and-white films. Outdoors the light is often so bright that even the smallest aperture used will lead to overexposure.

Tiffen Neutral Density Filters do not change the color of the light, therefore do not affect color rendition in color and black and white photography.

The table at the top of page 81 will help you choose the correct Tiffen Neutral Density Filter or combination of filters without having to resort to mathematics.

Where heavy neutral density filters are to be used on a reflex camera this may interfere with focusing. In such a situation focus with the same number of light-colored Tiffen filters, such as the skylight, on the lens as you are going to use for the finished picture. Shortly before exposure substitute the same number of Tiffen Neutral Density Filters needed to make the exposure.

When needed, other filter density combinations than those shown here may be made. When combining two or more Tiffen Neutral Density Filters the filter factors should be multiplied by each other. Thus a Tiffen ND1.0 plus a Tiffen ND.3 (2x) results in a filter factor of 20x.

TIFFEN NEUTRAL DENSITY FILTER SELECTOR CHART II

In outdoor pictorial work it is often desired to open the lens to a wide aperture in order to throw the background out of focus.

With modern fast color and black-and-white films this is often impossible, even when the highest shutter speed is used. The table at the bottom of page 81 shows which Tiffen Neutral Density Filter or combination of filters will enable you to open up to the desired aperture.

TIFFEN NEUTRAL DENSITY SELECTOR CHART I.

(Left axis: STOP FOR CORRECT EXPOSURE WITHOUT ND FILTER — Right axis: TIFFEN NEUTRAL DENSITY FILTER TO USE)

Smallest marked stop	f/16	f/22	f/32
f/22	ND.3 (x2)	NONE	NONE (use f/22)
f/32	ND.6 (x4)	ND.3 (x2)	NONE
f/45	ND.9 (x8)	ND.6 (x4)	ND.3 (x2)
f/64	ND.9 plus ND.3	ND.9 (x8)	ND.6 (x4)
f/90	ND.9 plus ND.6	ND.9 plus ND.3	ND.9 (x8)
f/128	ND.9 plus ND.9	ND.9 plus ND.6	ND.9 plus ND.3
f/180	ND1.0 plus ND1.0 plus ND.1	ND.9 plus ND.9	ND.9 plus ND.6
f/256	ND1.0 plus ND1.0 plus ND.4	ND1.0 plus ND1.0 plus ND .1	ND.9 plus ND.9

TIFFEN NEUTRAL DENSITY SELECTOR CHART II.
DESIRED APERTURE FOR SELECTIVE FOCUS

(Left axis: APERTURE WITHOUT TIFFEN ND FILTER)

	f/5.6	f/4	f/2.8	f/2 ND.9 and	f/1.4 ND.9 and
f/8	ND.3	ND.6	ND.9 ND.9 and	ND.3 ND.9 and	ND.6 ND.1 and
f/11	ND.6	ND.9	ND.3	ND.6	ND.9
f/16	ND.9	ND.9 and ND.3	ND.9 and ND.6	ND.4 and ND.9	ND1.0 and ND1.0 and ND.1
f/22	ND.9 and ND.3	ND.9 and ND.6	ND.9 and ND.1 / ND1.0 and	ND1.0 and ND1.0 and ND.1	
f/32	ND.9 and ND.6	ND.9 and MD.9	ND1.0 and ND.1		

NEUTRAL DENSITY FILTER TABLE

Type	Density	% Light Trans.	Increase in stop
ND.1	0.10	80	1/2
ND.2	0.20	63	3/4
ND.3 (x2)	0.30	50	1
ND.4	0.40	40	1 1/4
ND.5	0:50	32	1 3/4
ND.6 (x4)	0.60	25	2
ND.7	0.70	20	2 1/4
ND.8	0.80	16	2 3/4
ND.9 (x8)	0.90	13	3
ND.1.0 (x10)	1.00	10	3 1/4

Courtesy Tiffen Optical Co.

DECAMIRED SYSTEM

Decamired filters accomplish the same purpose as the light balancing and conversion Wratten 81 and 82 series previously discussed. But, they are somewhat easier to use since the whole system is arithmetic. By simple subtraction, you can determine the right filter or combination of filters to balance your color film with any light source.

The decamired number assigned to each film type and light source is, technically, determined by dividing the color temperature in degrees Kelvin into 1,000,000; and this divided by 10. The assigned decamired value of each filter indicates its ability to convert the light from a specific source to a desired color temperature.

There are a total of 8 or 10 decamired filters available, most sets consisting of a B1½, B3, B6, B12; R1½, R3, R6, R12. The B (blue) series, like the Wratten 82 series, in effect raises the color temperature of the source and has a cooling effect on the color of the transparency: The R (red) series, like the Wratten 81 series, effectively lowers the color temperature of the source and has a warming effect on the scene. The table on page 84 shows the decamired equivalents of light balancing and conversion filters; the table on page 83 shows decamired values assigned to your film and to some of the most common light sources.

DECAMIRED TABLE

Light Source	Decamired Value	Film Type
Candle or Kerosene Lamp Flame	52	
Carbon Filament Lamp	47	
Vacuum Tungsten Lamp or Acetylene Flame	42	
Household Tungsten Lamp 40-60 Watt	36	
100 Watt	35	
3200K Studio Type Tungsten Lamps	31	
Photoflood Lamps	29	Type A Kodachrome II
Warm-White Fluorescent Lamp	29	
Electric Arc, Solid Carbons	27	
Clear, Wire-Filled Flashlamps	26	
Cool-White Fluorescent Lamp	22	
Sunlight, before 9 AM, after 3 PM	20	
Sunlight, 9 AM to 3 PM (average)	18	Day'lt Type Kodachrome II
Electronic Flash	15	
Heavily Overcast Sky	15	
Lightly Overcast Sky	13	
Blue Sky, Hazy	11	
Blue Sky, In Shadow	8	
Blue Sky, Clear	4	

DECAMIRED EQUIVALENTS OF LIGHT BALANCING
AND CONVERSION FILTERS

Warming		Cooling	
REGULAR FILTER	APPROXIMATE EQUIVALENT	REGULAR FILTER	APPROXIMATE EQUIVALENT
81	R1	82	B1
81A	R2	82A	B2
81B	R3	82B	B3
81C	R3.5	82C	B4.5
81D	R4	82C+82	B5.5
81EF	R5	82C+82A	B6.5
85C	R8	82C+82B	B7.5
85	R11	82C+82C	B9
85B	R13	80C	B8
		80B	B11

It is possible to use your regular filters for color as Decamired filters, by re-labeling them as in this table. However, for most accurate results it's recommended you purchase a set of Decamired Filters.
From "Filter Guide" by Norman Rothschild and Cora Wright, published by Amphoto.

In practice, here's how it works. First of all, the filters within either series can be used in combination to produce almost any desired shift. An R6 plus an R12, for example, gives you an R18. Now, look at the chart on page 85. Suppose you are shooting Kodachrome II Daylight Type (decamired value 18) under a light overcast sky (decamired value 13). The difference is 5, and since the decamired value of the light source is less than the decamired value of your film, you would use the R series to lower the color temperature of the light source. Since you probably do not have a filter specifically designated R5, you would use an R3 and R1½ in combination, to match film and source as closely as possible. Where there is a choice between a somewhat higher or lower filter than the calculated density, choose the lower density, provided it is not more than one number lower.

Now, suppose you are shooting available light, with regular 100-watt household bulbs as the sole sources and Kodachrome II Type A in your camera. The decamired value for the film is 29; for the source, 35. The difference is 6, and since in this case the value of the light source is greater than the value for your film, you would use the B series to raise the color temperature of the light source, specifically the B6 filter.

If you shoot against the light with Kodachrome II, you can hold shadow detail without burning out highlights. Kodachrome II Daylight Type, exposure 1/60 and f/5.6. Photograph by Viereck, with Zeiss Ikon camera.

While this table covers a number of situations, you will find that a color temperature meter will be a great aid in using these filters. A meter which reads directly in decamired values, such as the Gossen Sixticolor Temperature Meter, the Lifacolor Meter or the Rebikoff, is easiest, although of course color temperature in degrees Kelvin can be converted into decamired equivalents.

While the decamired system is simpler to use, the critical color worker will probably prefer the Kodak Wratten 81 and 82 series, since with the light balancing filter it isn't necessary to use more than two filters in combination, and image sharpness is affected by the addition of filters. The general rule is, the fewer the better.

HOW TO COMBINE FILTERS

You may find that you want to use several different filters in combination. If so, there are two points to keep in mind.

1) Filter factors. When using more than one filter, the filter factors should be multiplied. For instance: if you are combining a polarizing filter with a filter factor of 3X and a CC-50R filter with a filter factor of 2X, the factor for the combination would be 6X.

2) Order. For best results, a specific order should be followed. In general, the regular filter (Wratten 81, 82, or CC, among others) is farthest from the lens, and is preceeded by the polarizing filter and close-up lens (Chapter 8), in that order. Be sure to watch for vignetting when using a number of filters or attachments over the lens. It may be necessary to use the next largest series size, with a step-up ring.

TYPES OF FILTERS

Basically, there are three types of filters available for your camera: gelatin, cemented gelatin between optical glass, and solid glass. Each type has certain advantages—and disadvantages—as follows:

1) Gelatin. These filters are very thin, hence have practically no effect on image (decreasing sharpness, shifting focus) even when used in combination. In addition, they are inexpensive. However, they can be very easily damaged, accidentally or in cleaning, and are meant for one—or with care—several uses.

2) Gelatin cemented between optical glass. These are easy to handle, to clean, and come in a wide variety of types and colors. However, since each filter has a total of four glass surfaces, they have more of an effect on focus and sharpness than either gelatin or glass filters. If properly cared for, these filters last indefinitely; if mishandled, they may come apart.

3) Glass. Here, the dye is actually added to the liquid glass, which is then poured into thin sheets, cooled, cut and bound into filters. These filters have good stability, are easy to handle and clean. They're better than cemented gelatin filters if they are to be used in combination, since they have only two surfaces per filter. However, dye color and hence absorption characteristics are more difficult to control than with gelatin.

Warning: do not use acetate filters meant for use in a light beam for color printing over the camera's lens. They are not up to optical quality, and will cause a loss of sharpness if used in this way.

A word about the glass used in filters. While it is all of high optical quality, there are differences from manufacturer to manufacturer. Some filters may be obtained in two types of glass. "B" glass is suitable for all general photographic work, including extreme close-ups and photomicrography (photographing through a microscope). "A" glass is superior, and of higher quality. In general with filters, you get what you pay for. And keep in mind that the manufacturer's recommendations as to exposure increase, and specific effect on color film should be used as a starting point only. When you first start to use a filter—any filter—I suggest that you keep careful notes as to light conditions, exposure (try bracketing), and shoot one exposure as you would without a filter. Then, gradually, you will learn what to except at different times, and what the filter can do for you under varying conditions.

There are several methods of attaching filters to your camera. Some filters are meant to be fitted directly onto the camera's lens:

they screw in, bayonet on, push on. Any method is acceptable provided you can still use a lens hood, which is desirable under any circumstances, but mandatory with filters, since without a hood they are further out than the front lens element, and are more likely to cause reflections or flare when hit by stray light.

A more versatile, and useful, system of attaching filters is the series size method. Eastman Kodak Co. and other major manufacturers all market filters to be used in this fashion. In practice, it makes it possible to break down filters to fit the infinite number of lens diameters on the market into about ten different standard sizes, series 4 through 11. These filters fit in adapter rings which attach to the camera's lens. The adapter rings are made in many sizes to fit the various diameter lenses, but the filters themselves remain the same, within one series size. The outer ring of many adapter rings may be replaced by a screw-in lens shade, which also serves to hold the filter in place. You can use the same filters for all lenses of similar size. Adapter rings are available in screw-in, bayonet, push-on, and set-screw types. Which you will need depends on the specific camera you have. If you have lenses of several different diameters, you may be best off buying filters in the series size to fit the largest lens. By using step-up rings, you will be able to use these filters with lenses which otherwise would require filters one series size smaller.

Unfortunately, while a number of manufacturers — Eastman Kodak Co., Tiffen, Enteco, Accura, Walz, Ednalite, Lifa, Harrison and Harrison, and various and sundry individual camera manufacturers—all market filters, the same or similar filters do not have the same name. A reliable photographic dealer should be able to advise you on this subject, and to help you get the precise filter you are after. An excellent book on the subject is *Filter Guide* by Norman Rothschild and Cora Wright (Amphoto).

LENS SHADES

You should use a lens shade at all times, indoors or out, to prevent stray light from hitting the lens surface and prevent flare and reflections. Shades come in a number of sizes, shapes, depths, and the most important thing to remember is to watch out for vignetting. If you are using a wide-angle lens, you may need a shorter shade than if the lens were of normal focal length, because the corners of your image may be cut off. Your photographic dealer will have information as to which shade is recommended by the various manufacturers for your specific lens.

Millipede on leaf was photographed by Herbert Keppler with Miranda C on copying stand, 135mm Schneider Tele-Xenar, plus 3 close-up lens, electronic flash. For a simple method of using electronic flash with Kodachrome II Daylight Type for closeups, see pages 98-100.

CHAPTER EIGHT

Close-ups

There are basically two methods of shooting close-ups: which is best for you depends on your camera and or how close you want to come to the subject. If yours is not an interchangeable-lens camera, you will have to use close-up lenses. If you can remove the lens from your camera, you may still find it convenient to use close-up lenses when you're not shooting extreme close-ups, but you will want extension tubes or bellows if you plan to come extremely close.

Close-up lenses are available from a number of different manufacturers in different series sizes to fit different size lenses. Those made by Eastman Kodak are called Porta lenses. They can be attached to the camera by means of an adapter ring as outlined in Chapter 7 on Filters. If you are using a filter together with a close-up lens, be sure that you have them in the proper order. In general, the close-up lens should be placed next to the camera's lens. For information on the use of close-up lenses, with still cameras, see the chart on page 92 which describes working distance from subject with various footage settings on the camera and the field covered for 50mm lenses. For information on using close-up lenses with 25mm and 13mm normal focal length lenses on 16mm and 8mm movie cameras, see the chart on page 103. For information on close-up lenses to be used with 13mm fixed focus lenses on 8mm cameras, see the chart on page 101.

EXTENSION TUBES AND BELLOWS

For close-up work (which we will consider anything closer than the camera's normal focusing range) you will find using a single-lens reflex camera or a reflex housing for your interchange-

CLOSE UP LENS (diopters)	Footage Setting on Camera	Inches from Subject to Lens	FIELD COVERED 50mm Lens 24 x 36mm Negative
+1	Inf.	38¾	18⅝ x 28
	50	37	17¾ x 26⅝
	25	34¾	16⅝ x 25
	"FIXED"	33¾	16 x 24
	15	32⅜	15⅜ x 23
	10	29⅝	14 x 21
	8	27⅞	13⅛ x 19¾
	6	25½	11⅞ x 17⅞
	5	23¾	11 x 16⅝
	4	21⅝	10 x 15
	3½	20⅜	9¼ x 14
+2	Inf.	19½	9⅜ x 14
	50	19⅛	9⅛ x 13⅝
	25	18½	8⅞ x 13¼
	"FIXED"	18	8⅝ x 12⅞
	15	17¾	8½ x 12¾
	10	16⅞	8 x 12
	8	16⅜	7¾ x 11½
	6	15½	7¼ x 10⅞
	5	14⅞	6⅞ x 10⅜
	4	14	6½ x 9⅝
	3½	13⅜	6⅛ x 9¼
+3	Inf.	13	6¼ x 9⅜
	50	12⅞	6⅛ x 9¼
	25	12½	5⅞ x 8⅞
	"FIXED"	12⅜	5⅞ x 8⅞
	15	12¼	5¾ x 8¾
	10	11⅞	5⅝ x 8⅜
	8	11½	5⅜ x 8⅛
	6	11⅛	5⅛ x 7⅞
	5	10¾	4⅞ x 7½
	4	10⅜	4¾ x 7⅛
	3½	10	4½ x 6⅞
+4 (3 + 1)	Inf.	9⅞	4⅝ x 7
	"FIXED"	9½	4½ x 6⅝
	3½	8	3⅝ x 5⅜
+5 (3 + 2)	Inf.	7⅞	3¾ x 5⅝
	"FIXED"	7⅝	3½ x 5⅜
	3½	6½	3 x 4⅜
+6 (3 + 3)	Inf.	6½	3 x 4⅝
	"FIXED"	6⅜	3 x 4⅜
	3½	5⅝	2½ x 3¾
+8	Inf.	5⅛	2¼ x 3⅜
	4	4⅝	2 x 3
+10	Inf.	4¼	1⅞ x 2¾
	4	4	1⅝ x 2½

Courtesy Tiffen Optical Co.

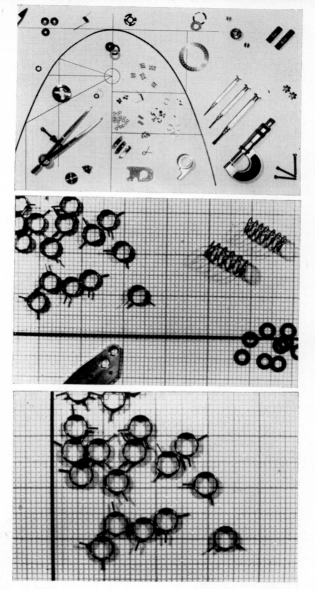

Three photographs made with the same camera (Contarex) and same lens (50mm f/2 Zeiss Planar). Top, from a distance of 35 inches; center, with close-up lens; bottom, with bellows attachment. Photographs by M. Meuer.

Tables for close-ups with focal distance lenses of 50 mm and 58 mm

	For lens focal distance of 50 mm						For lens focal distance of 58 mm					
Length of extension (mm)	Subject to lens distance (mm)	Lens to film distance (mm)	Subject to film distance (mm)	Ratio of reproduction	Area seen by lens (mm)	Exposure increase	Subject increase distance to lens (mm)	Lens to film distance (mm)	Subject to film distance (mm)	Ratio of reproduction	Area seen by lens (mm)	Exposure increase
0	∞	50	∞	varies*	varies*	1,0	∞	58	∞	varies*	varies*	1,0
5	550	55	605	0,1	240 x 360	1,2	731	63	794	0,09	267 x 400	1,2
10	300	60	360	0,2	120 x 180	1,4	394	68	462	0,17	141 x 212	1,4
15	217	65	282	0,3	80 x 120	1,7	282	73	355	0,26	92 x 138	1,6
20	175	70	245	0,4	60 x 90	2,0	226	78	304	0,35	69 x 103	1,8
25	150	75	225	0,5	48 x 72	2,3	192	83	275	0,43	56 x 84	2,1
30	133	80	213	0,6	40 x 60	2,6	170	88	258	0,52	46 x 69	2,3
35	121	85	206	0,7	34 x 51	2,9	154	93	247	0,60	40 x 60	2,6
40	113	90	203	0,8	30 x 45	3,2	142	98	240	0,69	35 x 52	2,9
45	106	95	201	0,9	27 x 40	3,6	133	103	236	0,78	31 x 46	3,2
50	100	100	200	1,0	24 x 36	4,0	125	108	233	0,86	28 x 42	3,5
55	95	105	200	1,1	22 x 33	4,4	119	113	232	0,95	25 x 40	3,8
60	92	110	202	1,2	20 x 30	4,8	114	118	232	1,03	23 x 35	4,1
70	86	120	206	1,4	17 x 26	5,8	106	128	234	1,21	20 x 30	4,9
80	81	130	211	1,6	15 x 23	6,8	100	138	238	1,38	17 x 26	5,7
90	78	140	218	1,8	13 x 20	7,8	95	148	243	1,55	15 x 23	6,5
100	75	150	225	2,0	12 x 18	9,0	92	158	250	1,72	14 x 21	7,4
110	73	160	233	2,2	11 x 16	10,2	89	168	257	1,90	13 x 19	8,4
120	71	170	241	2,4	10 x 15	11,6	86	178	264	2,07	12 x 17	9,4
130	69	180	249	2,6	9 x 14	13,0	84	188	272	2,24	11 x 16	10,5
140	68	190	258	2,8	9 x 13	14,4	82	198	280	2,41	10 x 15	11,7
150	67	200	267	3,0	8 x 12	16,0	80	208	288	2,60	9 x 14	12,9
160	66	210	276	3,2	8 x 11	17,6	79	218	297	2,76	9 x 13	13,8
170	65	220	285	3,4	8 x 11	19,4	78	228	306	2,92	8 x 12	15,5
180	64	230	294	3,6	7 x 10	21,2	77	238	315	3,09	8 x 12	16,8
190	63	240	303	3,8	6 x 9	23,0	76	248	324	3,26	7 x 11	18,3
200	63	250	313	4,0	6 x 9	25,0	75	258	333	3,44	7 x 10	19,8

Courtesy Amphoto, from "Miranda Manual."

	For lens focal distance of 100 mm						For lens focal distance of 135 mm					
Length of extension (mm)	Subject to lens distance (mm)	Lens to film distance (mm)	Subject to film distance (mm)	Ratio of reproduction	Area seen by lens (mm)	Exposure increase	Subject to lens distance (mm)	Lens to film distance (mm)	Subject to film distance (mm)	Ratio of reproduction	Area seen by lens (mm)	Exposure Increase
0	∞	100	∞	var-ies*	varies*	1,0	∞	135	∞	var-ies*	varies*	1,0
5	2100	105	2205	0,05	480 x 720	1,1	3780	140	3920	0,04	600 x 900	1,1
10	1100	110	1210	0,10	240 x 360	1,2	1958	145	2103	0,07	343 x 514	1,2
15	767	115	882	0,15	160 x 240	1,3	1350	150	1500	0,11	218 x 327	1,2
20	600	120	720	0,20	120 x 180	1,4	1046	155	1201	0,15	160 x 240	1,3
25	500	125	625	0,25	96 x 144	1,6	864	160	1024	0,19	126 x 189	1,4
30	433	130	563	0,30	80 x 120	1,7	742	165	908	0,22	109 x 164	1,5
35	386	135	521	0,35	69 x 103	1,8	656	170	826	0,26	92 x 138	1,6
40	350	140	490	0,40	60 x 90	2,0	591	175	766	0,30	80 x 120	1,7
45	322	145	467	0,45	53 x 80	2,1	540	180	720	0,33	73 x 109	1,8
50	300	150	450	0,50	48 x 72	2,3	500	185	685	0,37	65 x 97	1,9
55	282	155	437	0,55	44 x 65	2,4	466	190	656	0,41	59 x 88	2,0
60	267	160	427	0,60	40 x 60	2,6	439	195	634	0,44	55 x 82	2,1
70	243	170	413	0,70	34 x 51	2,9	395	205	600	0,52	46 x 69	2,3
80	225	180	405	0,80	30 x 45	3,2	363	215	578	0,59	41 x 61	2,5
90	211	190	401	0,90	27 x 40	3,6	338	225	563	0,67	36 x 54	2,8
100	200	200	400	1,00	24 x 36	4,0	317	235	552	0,74	32 x 49	3,0
110	191	210	401	1,10	22 x 33	4,4	301	245	546	0,82	29 x 44	3,3
120	183	220	403	1,20	20 x 30	4,8	287	255	542	0,89	27 x 40	3,6
130	177	230	407	1,30	18 x 27	5,3	275	265	540	0,96	25 x 38	3,9
140	171	240	411	1,40	17 x 26	5,8	265	275	540	1,04	23 x 35	4,2
150	167	250	417	1,50	16 x 24	6,3	257	285	542	1,11	21 x 32	4,5
160	163	260	423	1,60	15 x 23	6,8	249	295	544	1,18	20 x 30	4,8
170	159	270	429	1,70	14 x 21	7,3	242	305	547	1,26	19 x 29	5,1
180	156	280	436	1,80	13 x 20	7,8	236	315	551	1,33	18 x 27	5,4
190	153	290	443	1,90	13 x 19	8,4	231	325	556	1,41	17 x 26	5,8
200	150	300	450	2,00	12 x 18	9,0	226	335	561	1,48	16 x 25	6,2

Courtesy Amphoto, from "Miranda Manual."

able lens rangefinder camera most convenient. The reason: These have no parallax error, the finder image being formed by the camera lens. With any camera, still or movie, which does not feature through-the-lens viewing and focusing, the difference in point of view between viewfinder and camera lens becomes an increasingly difficult problem as you come closer to your subject. It is practically insurmountable in close-up work unless you are doing straight copying with a still camera, or working with a titler in movies, in which case there are devices made expressly for those purposes. With copy stands and titlers (instructions accompany them) you can be certain of exactly what is in the frame; however, it is always simpler to compose the picture while looking through a regular viewfinder, or ideally for close-ups through the lens.

Reflex housings for 35mm cameras are available from a number of manufacturers: Kilfitt, Novoflex, Nikon, Accura, E. Leitz, Canon, and Astro. Adapters are available which will fit most of these to almost any interchangeable-lens rangefinder camera on the market.

There are far, far too many different sets of extension tubes and bellows for us to cover them in detail here. Chances are that your camera's manufacturer makes extension tubes and bellows expressly for use with that camera. There are also a number of units available from general photographic manufacturers and importers. Accura imports a bellows unit which is both easy to use and inexpensive, costing about $30.

EXPOSURE

The greatest problem in making close-ups with tubes and bellows is in calculating exposure (no exposure increase is necessary with close-up lenses, since lens-to-film distance is not increased). Pick up your camera and focus the lens at infinity. Now, slowly turn the focusing mechanism to the closest focusing distance. You will notice that the distance from the lens to the camera gradually increases. The f/stop markings on your camera were calculated for the lens at infinity. Moving the lens forward to focus on closer objects decreases the light and also changes the marked f/stop value. The fall off is so slight that it will not appreciably affect your results at ordinary working distances. When you insert extension tubes or bellows between lens and camera for close-ups, the fall off is usually sufficient to cause underexposure unless you take it into account when calculating exposure. For your convenience, we have included close-up tables for focal lengths of 50, 58, 100, and 135mm lenses which cover a range of extension lengths. But just in case you have to calculate exposure increase, here's a step-by-step description of how to do it with any lens on any camera.

1. Find the actual diameter of the lens opening.

$$\text{Diameter} = \frac{\text{focal length}}{\text{marked } f/\text{stop}}$$

2. Find the effective aperture based on this diameter.

$$\text{Effective aperture} = \frac{\text{lens to film distance}}{\text{diameter}}$$

You may prefer to calculate the exposure factor (number of times exposure must be increased) as a basic method for shooting closeups.

$$\text{Exposure factor} = \frac{(\text{lens to film distance})^2}{(\text{focal length of lens})^2}$$

Since light fall off is so great when you are shooting extreme close-ups, you will often need to use auxiliary lighting equipment. Any of the types of illumination described in Chapter 6 on artificial light will do, of course, but probably the one best for many types of close-up work you want to do is electronic flash. (You may want to use tungsten lights, however, for focusing and composing, and to plan your exact lighting.) Electronic flash is particularly good for photographing flowers, insects, etc., since floods will heat up too rapidly. Circular electronic flash units which mount on the camera's lens are popular for close-ups in color. They flood the subject with even, shadowless light. Such units are made by Mighty Lite, Ascor, Graflex, Exakta, Hershey and Heiland. The charts on pages 98, 99, 100 describe exactly how to calculate exposure for flash or electronic flash simply, without recourse to the above method.

FIRST FIND YOUR SCALE OF REPRODUCTION

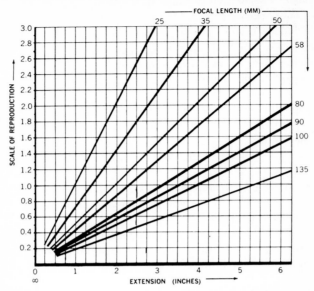

1. Find the diagonal line representing your lens focal length. Measure extension lens belond ∞ position (that is, length of extension tube or bellows used between lens and camera body). Read reproduction scale at left. Above 1.0 is bigger than life.

HOW TO USE FLASH FOR CLOSE UPS

If you shoot close-ups with bellows or extension tubes and flash (electronic or otherwise), you can use these tables and throw away all the rules on close-up calculations, depth of field and effective working aperture. You have two methods of working, depending on the magnification of your image. If you're producing an image on the film greater than life-size you can use the nomographs and chart here to figure your exposure to the letter. For close-ups with less magnification, there is an even more convenient method which eliminates any need of computations or use of charts. In the wide range of scale or reproduction from 0.2 to 1.0 (1:5 to 1:1) you can work with the same f-number regardless of the magnification used. Just fasten the flashlamp on the camera so that its distance from the film plane just about equals the focal length of the camera lens. Then, with increasing bellows extensions and magnifications, the increasing loss of effective lens speed

THEN GET THE LAMP-TO-SUBJECT DISTANCE

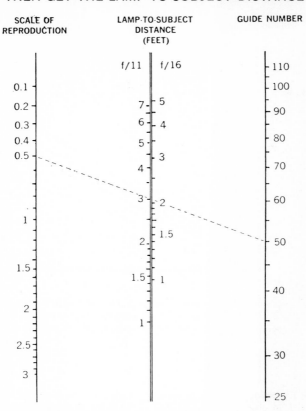

SCALE OF
REPRODUCTION

LAMP-TO-SUBJECT
DISTANCE
(FEET)

GUIDE NUMBER

2. Connect reproduction scale found in (1) with guide number of your flash. Read lamp-to-subject distance for f/11 or f/16 at center. Example: if reproduction scale is 0.5 and guide number is 50, lamp-to-subject distance is 3 ft. at f/11, 2.1 ft. at f/16.

is compensated by the automatic shortening of the lamp-to-subject distance. This will only work with a lens of 100mm focal length or greater. If you use a shorter lens, the lamp-to-subject distances will be to small. Best choice is a 135mm ens. To use nomographs opposite, lay a straight edge across the nomograph so that it touches two known values—e.g. scale of reproduction and flash guide number in chart 2. Then the unknown value—here, lamp-to-subject distance—will be given at the point where the straight edge crosses the center line. Courtesy Modern Photography. Nomographs copyrighted by Hermann Eisenbeiss.

NOW FIND YOUR DEPTH OF FIELD

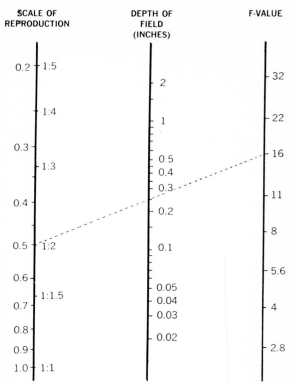

3. Align reproduction scale with working f/value to find depth of field. Here .5 (1:2) at f/16 gives you depth of field of .25 inches. This information, although not necessary for producing proper exposure, will indicate extent of sharpness.

If you are shooting close-ups without artificial light, the necessary exposure may run into seconds or even minutes. If this is the case, or for that matter if you will be making very long exposures for any other reason, you should shoot a test roll of Kodachrome II to determine its reciprocity failure.

The reciprocity law states that as long as the exposure (light intensity X time) is constant, the effect on a photographic emulsion will be the same. In actual practice, however, photographic emulsions, Kodachrome II included, do not react in accord with the law when exposure time is either very long or very short. Your Kodachrome II is constructed to produce the best color results when exposed for approximately 1/50 sec. You won't be able to see the difference if you expose it at, say ½ sec., or 1/500 sec. But if your exposure time is as long as a minute or as short as 1/10,000 you may run into trouble. With extremely long exposures, exposure times up to 3X that predicted on the basis of a meter reading may be necessary, and there may be color shifts. Data on reciprocity effect is generally not published since the actual effect on speed and color balance may vary from not only one color product to another, but also from one emulsion lot to another. In general, with Kodachrome II, the shift will probably be for exposures of extremely long duration towards a slight cyan balance and some loss of speed. Accordingly, for these exceptional situations necessitating long exposures the best procedure is to bracket exposures on your first roll, giving 2X and 4X more than should be correct.

If it is possible, you will want to use a longer than normal focal length lens for extreme close-ups. With normal and wide-angle lenses, you will be too close to your subject. If longer than normal lenses are useful for almost all close-up work, they are practically essential with live subjects or if you want to use artificial illumination, watch the position of your shadow and the camera's when shooting. It is all too easy to cast a shadow over the area that you are photographing and not even notice it, throwing exposure calculations made on the basis of direct illumination off the beam.

DATA ON KODAK PORTRA LENSES WITH FIXED-FOCUS 8mm CAMERAS

	Range of Sharpness in Inches At Lens Setting of 8 (f/8)		Area Covered by Lens in Inches At Lens Setting of 8 (f/8)	
	From	To	Near	Far
Portra 1+	23	60	5½x7	15x20
Portra 2+	14	24½	3½x4¾	6⅛x8¼
Portra 3+	10¼	15¼	2¾x3⅝	3⅞x5⅛

Reproduced with permission from the copyrighted Kodak booklet "How to Make Good Home Movies," p. 171.

FIELDS OF VIEW IN INCHES FOR CLOSE-UP LENSES WITH ZOOM LENSES FOCUSED AT INFINITY

Diopter of close-up lens	+1	+2	+3	+4	+5	+6	+7	+8	+9	+10
Subject-to-CU-lens distance	39 1/2 in.	19 3/4 in.	13 in.	9 3/4 in.	8 in.	6 1/2 in.	5 1/2 in.	5 in.	4 1/2 in.	4 in.
Zoom focal length 8mm	16 1/8 x 21	8 1/16 x 10 1/2	5 3/8 x 7	4 1/16 x 5 1/4	3 1/4 x 4 3/16	2 11/16 x 3 1/2	2 5/16 x 3	2 x 2 5/8	1 13/16 x 2 5/16	1 5/8 x 2 1/8
9mm	14 3/8 x 18 11/16	7 3/16 x 9 5/16	4 3/4 x 6 1/4	3 9/16 x 4 11/16	2 7/8 x 3 3/4	2 3/8 x 3 1/8	2 1/16 x 2 11/16	1 13/16 x 2 5/16	1 9/16 x 2 1/16	1 7/16 x 1 7/8
10mm	12 15/16 x 16 13/16	6 7/16 x 8 7/16	4 5/16 x 5 5/8	3 1/4 x 4 3/16	2 9/16 x 3 3/8	2 3/16 x 2 13/16	1 7/8 x 2 3/8	1 5/8 x 2 1/8	1 7/16 x 1 7/8	1 5/16 x 1 11/16
11.5mm	11 1/4 x 14 5/8	5 5/8 x 7 5/16	3 3/4 x 4 7/8	2 13/16 x 3 5/8	2 1/4 x 2 15/16	1 7/8 x 2 7/16	1 5/8 x 2 1/16	1 3/8 x 1 13/16	1 1/4 x 1 5/8	1 1/8 x 1 7/16
24mm	5 3/8 x 7	2 11/16 x 3 1/2	1 13/16 x 2 5/16	1 5/16 x 1 3/4	1 1/16 x 1 7/16	7/8 x 1 3/16	3/4 x 1	11/16 x 7/8	5/8 x 3/4	9/16 x 11/16
27mm	4 3/4 x 6 1/4	2 3/8 x 3 1/8	1 9/16 x 2 1/16	1 3/16 x 1 9/16	15/16 x 1 1/4	13/16 x 1 1/16	11/16 x 7/8	9/16 x 3/4	1/2 x 11/16	7/16 x 5/8
30mm	4 5/16 x 5 5/8	2 1/8 x 2 13/16	1 7/16 x 1 7/8	1 1/16 x 1 3/8	7/8 x 1 1/8	3/4 x 15/16	5/8 x 13/16	1/2 x 11/16	7/16 x 5/8	7/16 x 9/16
40mm	3 1/4 x 4 3/16	1 5/8 x 2 1/8	1 1/16 x 1 3/8	13/16 x 1 11/16	5/8 x 13/16	1/2 x 11/16	7/16 x 5/8	3/8 x 1/2	3/8 x 7/16	5/16 x 7/16

Courtesy Modern Photography (February 1961, p. 107).

DATA ON KODAK PORTRA LENSES FOR 16mm CAMERAS
with focusing 25mm lenses

Camera Focus Scale Setting in Feet	Portra Lens 2+		Portra Lens 3+	
	Portra Lens-to-Subject Distance in Inches	Area Covered By Lens in Inches	Portra Lens-to-Subject Distance in Inches	Area Covered By Lens in Inches
INF.	19½	5⅝x7½	13	3¾x5
50	19⅛	5⅜x7¼	12⅞	3⅝x4⅞
25	18½	5¼x7	12½	3½x4¾
15	17¾	5x6¾	12¼	3½x4⅝
10	16⅞	4¾x6⅜	11⅞	3⅜x4½
8	16⅜	4⅝x6¼	11½	3¼x4⅜
6	15½	4⅜x5⅞	11⅛	3⅛x4⅛
4	14	4x5⅜	10⅜	2⅞x3⅞
3	12⅝	3½x4⅝	9½	2¾x3⅝
2	10½	3x4	8¼	2⅜x3¼

DATA ON KODAK PORTRA LENSES FOR 8mm CAMERAS
with focusing 13mm lenses

Camera Focus Scale Setting in Feet	Portra Lens 2+		Portra Lens 3+	
	Portra Lens-to-Subject Distance in Inches	Area Covered By Lens in Inches	Portra Lens-to-Subject Distance in Inches	Area Covered By Lens in Inches
INF.	19½	5x6¾	13	3⅜x4½
50	19⅛	4⅞x6½	12⅞	3⅜x4⅜
25	18½	4¾x6⅜	12½	3¼x4⅜
15*	17¾	4⅝x6⅛	12¼	3¼x4¼
10	16⅞	4⅜x5⅞	11⅞	3⅛x4⅛
8	16⅜	4¼x5⅝	11½	3x4
6	15½	4x5⅜	11⅛	2⅞x3⅞
4	14	3⅝x4⅞	10⅜	2⅝x3½
3	12⅝	3¼x4⅜	9½	2½x3⅜
2	10½	2¾x3⅝	8¼	2¼x3

*The data for 15 feet apply to fixed-focus 8mm movie cameras.

Reproduced with permission from the copyrighted Kodak booklet "How to Make Good Home Movies," p. 174.

LENS SETTINGS FOR SLOW-MOTION CAMERA SPEEDS

When recom- mended setting at 16 Frames is:	USE SETTINGS BELOW AT			
	64 Frames	48 Frames	32 Frames	24 Frames
11	5.6	5.6–8	8	8–11
8	4	4–5.6	5.6	5.6–8
5.6	2.7 or 2.8	2.7–4 or 2.8–4	4	4–5.6
4	1.9 or 2	2–2.7 or 2–2.8	2.7 or 2.8	2.7–4 or 2.8–4
2.7 or 2.8	1.4	1.4–1.9 or 1.4–2	1.9 or 2	2–2.7 or 2–2.8

Each hyphenated setting is halfway between numbers shown.
Reproduced with permission from the copyrighted Kodak booklet "How to Make Good Home Movies," p. 103.

DEPTH OF FIELD

Depth of field is a major consideration in close-up work. Here, the added speed of Kodachrome II will be an aid, for you can shoot at an f/number approximately two times smaller than is possible with Kodachrome. When shooting close-ups with reflex viewing, stop your lens down to check depth of field on the ground glass before shooting. You will be able to do this either with single-lens reflexes or with rangefinder cameras and reflex housings.

Motion presents another problem in close-up photography. You will need to use a fairly high shutter speed to stop the motion of flowers moved by the most gentle breeze, or the progress of the most lethargic insect across a pebble or leaf (and many insects are anything but lethargic). Here, again, electronic flash is extremely useful: in this case, for stopping motion.

CHAPTER NINE

From Dealer's Shelf to Screen

There are a number of considerations other than the shooting techniques discussed in the preceding chapters which will contribute to the quality of your transparencies or length of movie footage as you view them. To mention a few: care of undeveloped film before and after processing, care of processed film, quality of projector, screen and image size, editing technique with both stills and movies.

PRECAUTIONS BEFORE PROCESSING

While the expiration date on your Kodachrome II film is accurate and actually includes a safety factor, this date assumes that the film has not been subjected to high heat or high humidity before processing. Prolonged storage under adverse conditions, may cause minor color shifts in your film.

The professional solution to this problem, and one which I would suggest that you adopt if you are keeping more Kodachrome II on hand than you will use within a few weeks, is to store all the unexposed film in the refrigerator. If you plan to keep the film for a very long period, you might even place it in the freezer. Frozen film remains stable for an indefinite number of years. Otherwise, keep the film in the regular section of the refrigerator. Wrap it in a plastic bag and place the bag in one of the plastic hydrators intended for keeping vegetables, available at any ten cent store. In this way you will keep the film out of the way of food (few of us are likely to go out and buy a special refrigerator just for film), and protect the film cartons from any accidental spillage. One word of caution: you must let the film warm up to room temperature before using it to take pictures. About 12 hours is the minimum recommended for frozen film; two to three hours is safe for film chilled to 35F. Do not unwrap the moisture-sealed paper package around the 35mm roll or take the tape from the movie film can before the film has warmed to room temperature. If you do, you risk condensation.

The combination of high heat and humidity, such as that common in tropical and semi-tropical areas, calls for extreme care in handling the film. One of the main problems is fungus growth. This is not a danger as long as film remains sealed in its original wrapper. But it can become acute when the film has been removed for exposure. If you plan to travel and photograph in areas in which such conditions are likely to be encountered, I suggest that you take a container which may be sealed against moisture (a sturdy plastic bag—just turn over the top after removing as much air as possible and twist tight with rubber bands—will do) with you in which to put all of your exposed film. Also, take a quantity of silica gel, a substance which absorbs moisture, to place with the film in the plastic bag. Actually drying the film requires a period of several days. Do not reseal exposed Kodachrome II which has been in humid conditions in its original container. Moisture can be removed from silica gel by heat: so if you have any reason to suspect that the gel has become saturated, simply heat in a 400° oven for about 30 minutes. Fungus, incidentally, can also damage cameras and lenses. When they are not in use, keep yours in moisture proof containers (if you don't have a special case, again plastic bags are an excellent substitute) with silica gel.

High heat alone can also cause a great deal of damage to your film in a short time. Do *not* leave your camera loaded with film in your car when it is parked in the sun. Glove compartment, trunk, back shelf, or seat—all reach an extremely high temperature in a matter of minutes on a hot summer day. Take the camera and any extra film you have out of the car with you.

Whether you are out on a day's expedition or on a long trip, you will find two types of insulated bags quite useful. One type is made for picnics or lunches; the other for carrying babies' bottles. The latter has a shoulder strap which comes in handy. If you are on a long trip in a hot climate, store exposed film in a large insulated bag. Load it into the bag at night when the temperature drops; keep the bag shut in daytime. Since insulated bags are available in a number of different sizes, you may decide that several small ones are more convenient for you than a single one. In a pinch, you might use the paper jiffy bags which are used to mail books, to pack ice cream and ice cubes, etc. The mouth of the bags can be folded over and sealed with tape. Ordinary newspaper actually gives effective insulation against heat. Use several layers wrapped individually around the load of film. The dead air spaces between the layers are the insulating element.

AFTER EXPOSURE: DOUBLE PRECAUTIONS

Exposed film is even more sensitive to adverse conditions than is film before exposure, since the latent image may be affected. The best rule is to have your film processed just as soon as possible. If you will be away from home for several months, arrange to ship your film back for processing directly to Eastman Kodak Co. You may purchase a prepaid processing mailer at any Kodak film dealer, the price of which is the processing charge. Your exposed film is then inserted in the mailer and dropped in the nearest mail box. It will be processed by one of Kodak's processing labs in the U.S. If you are travelling abroad, you may mail your film back directly to the U.S. Kodak lab or have it processed through a Kodak dealer overseas. If on a trip, it is easiest to purchase a mailer for each roll at the time you pick up your film so that you can send in each roll successively as it is exposed. The processed slides will be mailed to any address you specify. I like it because most of my slides are ready for viewing immediately upon my return home from a trip or vacation. If you purchase Kodachrome II outside the U.S., your purchase price will include the processing charges.

When packing film for mailing over long distances, you must be extremely careful. Put rolls (each in its original metal container) in a plastic bag, and place the bag in a cardboard box filling any extra space with lightly crumpled paper. Place this box in a larger box; there should be at least 2-3 in. leeway between each surface. Cover the bottom of the larger box with 2-3 in. of crumpled paper (foam rubber is better but not always readily available), center the box containing the film on this, stuff each side with crumpled paper or other shock-absorbing material and top with the same. Seal this box and mail it. The paper (or foam rubber) will help to insulate the film against extremes of heat or cold as well as absorbing shock which might jolt open the individual cassettes.

LOADING THE CAMERA

Since Kodachrome II is faster than Kodachrome, be certain never to load your camera in bright light. Light leaking into the cassette or into the sides of the movie roll will almost certainly streak the film. If you *must* load your camera outdoors, cover your head with a coat, blanket, or any over available material.

PROTECTING YOUR SLIDES

While your 35mm and 828 Kodachrome II slides will be returned beautifully mounted in cardboard and numbered in sequence from the processor, you should consider mounting them in glass if they will undergo much handling. Some projectors, however, will not accept regular glass mounts. Most of these however are automatic machines having slide trays from which the slides, once you have edited and arranged them to your satisfaction, may not have to be removed. These trays can be kept in special boxes and cases which may be dust porofed. Even so, you would be wise to consider other methods of additional protection against scratches, fingerprints, etc.

Plastic sleeves: thin plastic sleeves which slip over the slide, mount and all, are highly recommended. You can seal the edges with transparent tape to keep out dust. These fit in many projectors: but not in others (they cause jamming), so try one on a reject slide before placing them on all of your transparencies. Kimac Protectors are manufactured by the Kimac Co., 18 Mortimer Dr., Old Greenwich, Conn.

108

Plastic coating: Miracote is a solution in which you dip the slide in its mount. Since it is difficult to remove the slide from the mount once this is done, think twice if you want to have prints made later. Available at your photo dealer, manufactured by Foralco Enterprises, 307 W. 38th St., New York 18, N. Y.

Thin glass: Many slide projectors which won't accept regular glass mounts (this includes, particularly, many of the newer automatic machines, will take slides mounted in 3/32-in. thick glass. Masks are available from Eastman Kodak Co. Gemounts, Porter Mfg. & Supply Co., and the Kimac Co. all make special size masks (you can crop your slides) which are thin enough to be used. A number of companies supply thin glass mounts; Graflex, Inc.; Erie Scientific Corp.; Emde Products, Inc.; E. Leitz, Inc.; Karl Heitz, Inc.; and the Airequipt Mfg. Co. These mounts may be ordered through your photographic dealer. You cannot use regular slide binding tape with these mounts, since it is too thick. Special tape is required.

A number of types of regular mounts are available. The following is a rundown on types and techniques for using them, excerpted from an article by Norman Rothschild appearing in the October, 1961, issue of *Modern Photography*.

1) Glass Masks and Tape. The cheapest and most versatile way of getting the job done. Try odd shaped masks for cropping (see list above) your slides.

2) Binders that slide together. Easy to use. Simply slide the upper half of the binder into a groove in the lower half (with your slide sandwiched in between). However, these binders have a tendency to slide apart if the carrier springs are tight. This can be prevented by applying a small piece of cellulose tape across the open end of the binder frame.

3) Binders that snap together. These consist of an upper and lower metal frame. It is difficult to get curly film and glasses to stay put while the upper frame is snapped on. Try placing the transparency and glasses into the recess in the lower mount half. Hold in place with finger of left hand. Slip index finger of right hand into the opening in the upper mount half. Next lower this half into place, at the same time placing your right index finger on the glasses so they'll stay put. Now use your left hand to line up both halves. The entire assembly can now be picked up and snapped together.

4) Metal frame, masks, and glass. Offered only by Emde Products, Inc. Slip cardboard mount between two thin sheets of glass and slide into a metal frame. Then slide the whole assembly into place in a channel in the binder frame and close the mount by bending over the metal flap. Mounts are made in both metal and plastic.

5) Fiber and glass. Called Type-On, the binder consists of a fiber frame, glasses, and a gummed paper mask on which you can type or write identifying information. Should you accidentally drop a slide, the fiber will absorb the shock and minimize the risk of breakage. To use Type-On, wet one half of the mask and glue the frame into place. Insert one glass while the mask is still damp, put the transparency in place, and insert the second piece of glass. There is a paper flap which you must moisten and fold over to seal the mount.

Be sure to test your projector with a sample slide binder on one or two slides before investing in a large supply of the binders. Information on the specific manufacturers and their individual products will be available at your dealers.

VIEWING SLIDES

There are a number of methods of viewing your slides. For editing purposes, the best device is a transparency illuminator, such as the Kodak DeLuxe Transparency Illuminator, Model 2, commonly called a light box. A number of other illuminators are available as well, or you can construct your own. The most important considerations are color temperature of the light source (its light distribution should of course be even) and its spectral energy distribution. The illumination in the room in which the transparencies are to be viewed affects the necessary color temperature. In a dark room or one illuminated by low level tungsten light, the color temperature can be as low as 3200K; but if daylight enters the room your slides will look too blue. Even more important is the spectral distribution of the light, which should have the correct amounts of blue, green and red to relate to the absorbtions of the dyes used in the film. The Kodak illuminator mentioned above has a built-in filter which keeps illumination at about 3800K. The best solution, actually, is to have an illuminator which uses both tungsten and fluorescent lights as the source for highly critical work, or for displaying enlarged transparencies which can be made from your Kodachrome II 35mm and 828 slides. However, if you are planning to use a light box simply for screening your slides, planning their sequence for projection, and eliminating rejects, perfect color balance is not essential.

You will find a hand magnifier helpful in examining your slides on the light box, since difference in sharpness, in expression, in lighting are difficult to spot with the unaided eye.

No matter how complete the list of characteristics, a description of specific equipment such as a slide (or movie) projector is no substitute for actually going to a well-stocked camera store, examining the various machines, and having their operation demonstrated for you. Remember, as with any other photographic equipment, that while you get what you pay for, the features you get should be based on the features you want and need. There is little point in purchasing a machine with remote control focusing, reverse, forward, automatic timing mechanism, etc., if you are going to limit your slide showings to members of your own family within the confines of one 13 x 15 living room.

WHAT YOU NEED FOR MOVIES

The minimum of equipment that you need for viewing your movies is, of course, a projector. But if your movie making is to be more than simple documentation of family or trips, to be viewed 100 ft. roll after 100 ft. roll just as you shot it, you will also need a splicer and editor.

A movie editor can be tested easily and simply right at your photographic dealers. Some things to look for: good over-all construction; image sharpness and size; even illumination; ease of threading and removing the film for splicing; brightness sufficient for easy viewing in ordinary room light; storage considerations; size of rewind's arms (this determines size of reel which may be used);

111

PROJECTION DISTANCES AND PICTURE WIDTH

Projector-to-screen distance in feet	8mm projector 3/4" lens 16mm projector 1½" lens	8mm projector 1" lens 16mm projector 2" lens	16mm projector 3" lens
8	2'0"	1'6"	
10	2'6"	1'10"	1'3"
12	3'0"	2'3"	1'6"
16	4'0"	3'0"	2'0"
20	5'0"	3'9"	2'6"
25		4'8"	3'1"

Reproduced with permission from the copyrighted Kodak booklet "How to Make Good Home Movies," p. 81.

rewind gear ratio; rewind brakes to prevent backlash; type of splicer (tape or cement).

Editors range in price from about $6 to over $100, with price being an excellent guide to versatility and features.

Excellent movie projectors are made by Argus, Bell & Howell, Eastman Kodak Co., Keystone, and Mansfield, to mention just a few. Again, base your choice of projector on your needs. One point to check with any projector: how it handles your film. Take a roll of exposed film (not prize footage) with you when you go to select a projector. Run it through the machine at your dealer's, and examine it for scratches.

SCREENS

There are basically four types of screens available. One, the matte screen, offers a wide viewing angle but has the lowest reflectivity of any of the screen types and is not really suitable for images larger than about 30 x 30 in. unless you have a powerful projector. The second type, the metallic-surface screen, has very high reflectivity, but a narrow viewing angle. Viewers sitting a few feet to the side of the projector will see a much less brilliant image. Beaded screens, the third type, present an image which is brighter than a matte

PROJECTION DATA—MATTE AND BEADED SCREENS

Projector	Lens	Lamp Wattage	Matte Screen		Beaded Screen	
			Approximate Picture Width	Approximate Screen Distance	Approximate Picture Width	Approximate Screen Distance
8mm	¾-inch f/1.6	300	30 inches	11 feet	32 inches	11½ feet
		500	40 inches	15 feet	44 inches	15½ feet
	1-inch f/1.6	300	30 inches	15 feet	32 inches	15½ feet
		500	40 inches	20 feet	44 inches	21 feet
		750	3½ feet	22 feet	4 feet	23 feet
		1000	4 feet	25 feet	4½ feet	25 feet
16mm	2-inch f/1.6	300	5 feet	26 feet	5 feet	27 feet
		500	6 feet	32 feet	6½ feet	34 feet
		750	7 feet	36 feet	7½ feet	38 feet
		1000	8 feet	42 feet	8½ feet	45 feet

Reproduced with permission from the copyrighted Kodak booklet "How to Make Good Home Movies," p. 186.

screen but less bright than that of a metallic screen. Viewing angles are better than with a metallic screen, but not so wide as with matte screens. The tiny beads however, obscure the finest detail in your picture, which can be disturbing if the viewer is sitting too close to the screen—and seems a waste of the remarkable Kodachrome II sharpness. The newest, and probably the best, screens on the market have a lenticular surface, offering both a high reflectivity and wide viewing angle.

If you have a still camera, you will want a square screen so that you can project both verticals and horizontals; if your shooting is confined to movies, a horizontal screen will do.

Unless you have some space where a screen can be permanently placed, you will probably be interested in a tripod screen which can be folded up and stored in a closet. These are adjustable in height, and usually have carrying handles for easy portability. If you do have a permanent place to keep your screen, you should look into wall screens, which are available in a number of sizes, types, and at a wide range of prices. These screen manufacturers will be happy to send you information on their products: Aurora Industries, Inc., P.O. Box 6905, Chicago 80, Ill.; Bodde Screen and Projector Co., P.O.

Box 711, San Fernando, Calif.; Brumberger Sales Corp., 34-34th St., Brooklyn 32, N. Y.; Da-Lite Screen Co., Inc., Box 192, Warsaw, Ind.; Knox Mfg. Co., 9715 Soreng Ave., Schiller Park, Ill.; Raven Screen Corp., 124 E. 124th St., New York 35, N. Y.; Radiant Mfg. Corp., 8220 N. Austin Ave., Morton Grove, Ill.; Schultz Mfg. Co., 262-272 Johnston Ave., Jersey City 4, N. J.

The size screen you will need depends largely on where you anticipate projecting your slides, and to how large an audience. The usual size for most amateurs is about 40 x 40; however, if you will be giving slide shows at a camera club, or other organization, you may find a 50 x 50 or even a 60 x 60 screen is necessary. The actual image size you get on the screen will of course depend on focal length of the projector's lens and the projection distance. The farther the projector is from the screen, of course, the higher wattage lamp you will need in order to have a sufficiently bright image. The table on page 112 shows maximum distances for projecting 8 and 16mm movies for various lamp wattages, and the size image which the normal focal length lenses supplied on projectors will produce.

CHAPTER TEN

The Technical Story

Kodachrome was the first integral tri-pack color film available to the public, and it is understating the case to say that it has been a success. Undoubtedly, it has been the world's best selling color film. Although there have been a number of revisions in the film and the processing, you could always shoot at $f/6.3$ at 1/50 on a bright day and astonish the neighbors with your skill.

Even though the basic Kodachrome system of photography has not been changed, Kodachrome II is an improved film. It has superior speed, graininess and sharpness characteristics, and color rendition.

To provide an objective comparison of the two films, Kodak has furnished technical information on their characteristics. Since the measurements are derived from specific materials, with optimum processing, they cannot be considered as being exact for general usage. As with any production item a given sample may show slight variations from average values. Furthermore the new film, like its predecessor, will probably evolve slightly as techniques and technology advance.

Getting down to specifics, the change that is most apparent to the amateur between the two Kodachromes is speed. The new material is faster. Kodachrome II is rated by Kodak as having an Exposure Index of 25 for the daylight film (Kodachrome Type A is 16). The speed of the new film is ideal for obtaining good results in

115

bright sunlight with 8mm movie cameras, since few of these have smaller relative apertures than $f/16$, or speeds other than a nominal 1/30 sec. This worked out in our tests to a speed of 30 for the average sunlighted subject or 25 with due allowances for variables such as shutters, scene brightness, etc. (If a higher speed had been chosen for Kodachrome II, serious overexposure would have resulted when it was used in average equipment under average conditions.) The Type A speed was established so that conversion filters can be used conveniently. Undoubtedly, additional speed could have been obtained, but the potential was invested in quality.

The plot of density vs. log-relative exposure or the sensitometric curve of a black-and-white film describes the manner in which film reproduces the tones of various degrees of brightness of a test object. To describe the response of a three-color system, such as Kodachrome, it is necessary to plot three curves. In the case of color materials of this type it is customery to plot a different kind of density; the equivalent neutral density vs. relative-log exposure for each sensitive layer. This density describes the visual effectiveness of the dye deposits in each of the photosensitive layers (cyan density for the red sensitive layer, magenta density for the green sensitive layer, and yellow density for the blue sensitive layer). For a given exposure, the relative position of the points on the three curves indicates the appearance of a gray object. If the cyan point, for example, is higher than the others, the reproduction will be cyan rather than neutral.

Studies made on the reproduction of color in photographs show that it is not essential and often is not desirable to reproduce the gray scale as an absolute visual neutral. The optimum color balance is a compromise of many factors involving the preferred reproductions of many common colors including flesh, sky, water, grass and even grays which under some circumstances seem more acceptable when slightly cyan or blue than when slightly red or yellow in balance. Color temperature of projector illuminants further influences the choice of optimum color balance as does the color temperature of the illuminant used in making the exposure.

As shown by the sensitometric curves, it takes .40 log E less exposure to obtain a given medium density, say 1.0, with Type II

Kodachrome than with Type I Kodachrome; *i.e.*, Kodachrome II is 2½ times the speed of Kodachrome I. We may take pictures with Type II Kodachrome when the light is 40% of the level required for Kodachrome I. One may choose between stopping down by 1¼ stops or increasing shutter speed by a factor of 2½ times. All of these considerations are taken into account in the new exposure guides supplied with Kodachrome II.

The speed of Kodachrome II was increased to EI 25 and not some higher value in order to prevent serious overexposure of extreme situations of light subjects, bright sun and highly reflecting surroundings as in snow or beach scenes. In many amateur cine-8 cameras where the lowest exposure possible is 1/30 second at *f*/16, such scenes would be badly overexposed if the film speed was any more than EI 25. With film of EI 25 this equipment will produce only a slight overexposure. A film speed of EI 40 was established for Type II photoflood or Type A film, since it was considered desirable to maintain the EI 25 limit when exposed with the Type A to daylight conversion filter (Wratten 85).

The contrast relationship of Kodachrome II versus Kodachome can be illustrated by superimposing the magenta curves of the two films at the density of 1.0 point. The best contrast for a color film depends on many factors, among which are: (1) the realistic reproduction of relative brightness relationships in the scene with due allowance for camera and projector lens flare, (2) the beneficial effect of high contrast on color saturation, and (3) the beneficial effect of high contrast on picture sharpness. Basic improvements in sharpness and in dye systems have made it possible to reduce the contrast level to permit more pleasing tonal gradation, more detail in highlights, and more detail in the open shadows with Type II Kodachrome. Under some condtions, the low contrast of the film combined with extreme flare from a dirty lens will produce an objectionably flat result.

The increased latitude (range of exposure values over which tonal gradations can be recorded) of Type II Kodachrome results from the lower contrast. The increased latitude permits the amateur to get more acceptable results from over- and underexposures, especially those where the exposure is 1½ to 2 stops in error.

117

For the 8mm movie fan the most striking feature of the new Kodachrome system is the improvement in its optical and physical properties, *i.e.*, its sharpness and graininess. In the diagram on page 7, which is a diagrammatic sketch of the structure of Kodachrome II. we can see that this film includes an overcoat with interlayers between the photosensitive layers. The photosensitive layers in Kodachrome II are considerably thinner than in former films so that, even with the addition of interlayers, the total film thickness has been reduced appreciably. The use of new thing emulsion manufacturing techniques allows the total depth of gelatin to be reduced to about $2/3$ of the thickness found in Kodachrome film. The reduction in thickness of the photosensitive layer is an important factor in the improved sharpness of Kodachrome II.

On page 123 are manual tracings of a recording microdensitometer track at right angles to the image of a knife edge on each of the two films. The curves are shown superimposed. In both cases, white light was used for the exposure. The adjacency effect is more pronounced in the Kodachrome II trace. The slope of the Kodachrome II trace away from the vertical is less than the slope of Kodachrome in a ratio of about $1/2$. The total spread of the Kodachrome II trace is less than that of Kodachrome in a ratio of about $1/1.3$. In all three aspects, the data indicates that Kodachrome II is able to record an edge with a sharper demarcation than Kodachrome.

The practical tests corroborate this conclusion. Since Kodachrome is a very sharp film itself, and since the eye is capable of resolving only a certain amount of detail, the difference between the films in the larger formats, 16mm and 35mm, is nothing astonishing. But in the 8mm size it is a pleasant surprise. Some observers feel that the sharpness of an image produced by 8mm Kodachrome II comes very close to the sharpness of the same image produced by 16mm Kodachrome.

This impression is reinforced by the smoothness of the Kodachrome II image. One set of data herewith is from a common test for image smoothness or granularity: a microdensitometer trace across an area of uniform neutral (gray) middle density. Manual tracings of the fever charts from a recording microdensitometer with a 40 micron circular aperture were furnished. The peaks and valleys

118

indicate the extent of the variation from a perfectly even tone. The greatest variation for Kodachrome II is about .6 that of Kodachrome in these particular traces.

The image smoothness or grain of Kodachrome is so fine that there is a common, erroneous belief that it has no grain structure. (This belief is strengthened by knowledge of the fact that the silver is bleached out in the processing, but nevertheless there is a discontinuity in tone under high magnification.) In practice, the image smoothness of Kodachrome is enough to create the impression of perfection in the 16mm and 35mm formats under normal magnification. Under ordinary circumstances, a viewer would be hard put to distinguish image smoothness or sharpness between Kodachrome and Kodachrome II when comparing 35mm vs. 35mm. But, as already noted with respect to sharpness, the story with 8mm is quite different. An image produced by 8mm Kodachrome II compares very favorably with the same image produced by 16mm Kodachrome film, as the microdensitometer trace would predict. The transition from Kodachrome I to Kodachrome II film was accompanied by a change in the processing. The K-12 process recommended for Kodachrome II is different from the old Kodachrome process; it requires different chemicals and involves more steps. Neither film is compatible with the other's process.

The change in process permitted the introduction of improved combinations of new couplers (in the developing solutions) and new developing agents producing a new family of image dyes in the processed Type II Kodachrome film. For comparison purposes, the accompanying spectrophotometric curves for Kodachrome I and Kodachrome II show the densities of the individual dyes at each wavelength throughout the visible spectrum. Note in the case of the yellow dyes that both have an equal peak absorption in the blue (400-500) but that the Type II yellow dye absorbs much less green light. This situation indicates improvement, since yellow dyes are supposed to absorb blue light but not green light. Similarly, the Type II magenta dye absorbs less blue and red light, and the Type II cyan dye absorbs less green and blue light. The situation is summarized by the statement that the Type II dyes are sharper cutting, more selective, purer dyes. These changes in the dye absorption

119

characteristics are the major factors responsible for the improved color reproduction of Type II Kodachrome.

No data concerning the reciprocity failure of either the new or the old film were given by Kodak. Since Kodachrome II is designed for an exposure of about 1/50 sec., it may be assumed that very short exposure times such as encountered in high-speed motion pictures or very long exposure times such as used occasionally in copying or macro-photographic work will take their toll in sensitivity, lower contrast and disrupted layer balance. The general superiority of Kodachrome II should ameliorate any reciprocity failure effects to some extent, but only a test under actual conditions will get at the facts of the matter.

As with Kodachrome, the Eastman Kodak Company will not publish data about emulsion-number-to-emulsion-number differences. Their statements on the subject implied that the same or closer quality limits used for Kodachrome will be applied to Kodachrome II. For highly critical use, the photographer must test each new emulsion number in any case, so there is some doubt cast on the utility of publishing such information. Apparently the company feels that guesses from interpolated data lead to more bad pictures than does consistent technique in the face of minute product variations.

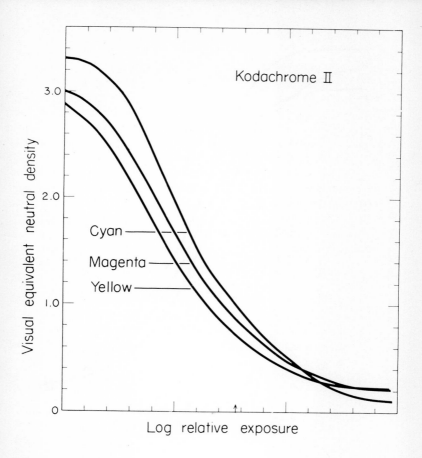

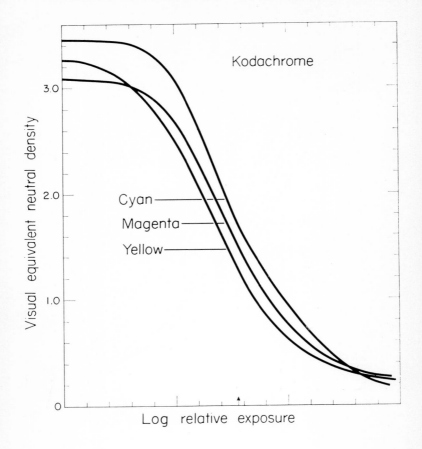

122

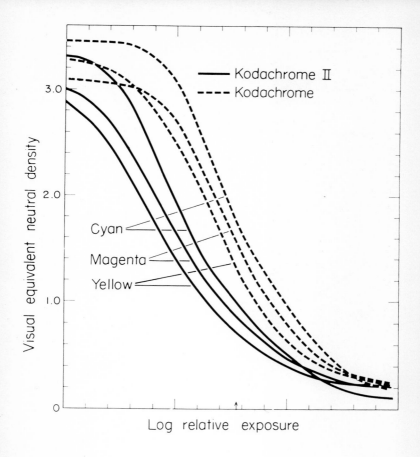

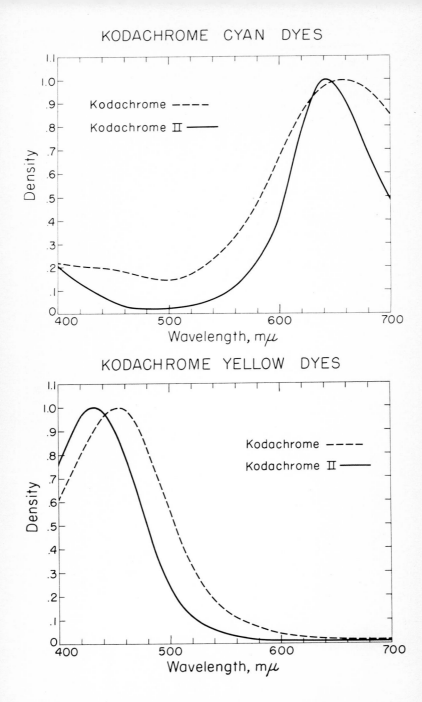

KODACHROME CYAN DYES

Kodachrome ----
Kodachrome II ——

Density

Wavelength, mμ

KODACHROME YELLOW DYES

Kodachrome ----
Kodachrome II ——

Density

Wavelength, mμ

KODACHROME MAGENTA DYES

Kodachrome - - - -
Kodachrome II ——

Density

Wavelength, mμ

Index